CW00520805

A World of Belts

Anne Leurquin

A World of Belts

*Africa, Asia, Oceania, America
from the Ghysels Collection*

Photos by
Mauro Magliani

Translation by Isabel Ollivier

Art Director
Marcello Francone

Editorial Coordination
Alessandra Chioetto

Editing
David Stanton

Layout
Serena Parini

The publisher thanks the Ghysels family
for allowing the publication of their collection,
and in particular Colette Ghysels
for the composition of the pictures and
the cooperation with the layout.

Note to the reader
*The size given is a belt's largest dimension
or the maximum dimension of the largest belt
in a group.*

First published in Italy in 2004 by
Skira Editore S.p.A.
Palazzo Casati Stampa
via Torino 61
20123 Milano
Italy
www.skira.net

Printed and bound in Italy. First edition

ISBN 88-8491-865-0

Distributed in North America and Latin America
by Rizzoli International Publications, Inc. through
St. Martin's Press, 175 Fifth Avenue, New York,
NY 10010.
Distributed elsewhere in the world by Thames
and Hudson Ltd., 181a High Holborn, London
WC1V 7QX, United Kingdom.

Contents

7   Introduction

11   Africa

105   Asia

241   Oceania

259   America

Captions

281   Africa
289   Asia
300   Oceania
302   America

Appendix

306   Maps
311   Glossary
313   Index
317   Bibliography

Introduction

Belts and *cache-sexe* are not trivial subjects, because they involve very different fields, including the particularly sensitive areas of sexuality and the concept of decency.

Margaret Mead's work is a significant example. Her fieldwork among ethnic groups in Samoa and New Guinea led to the publication of *Coming of Age in Samoa* (1928), followed by *Sex and Temperament in Three Primitive Societies* (1935), a set of studies of the Arapesh, Mundugumor and Tchambuli, whom she compared to the Samoans.

Mead tried to show the complexity of social, political and religious institutions, believing that by far the most complex rules of behaviour were those governing marital relations and sex because they laid the foundations for society as a whole.

Indeed, although belts are still used in most traditional ethnic groups, *cache-sexe* are now seldom worn except by a few rare groups whose survival is threatened, among other things, by the increasing tendency to fell equatorial forests.

The Jarawa on the Andaman Islands, an archipelago in the Indian Ocean, and all the tribes that live in the Amazon forest are cases in point.

But, fortunately, museums and private collectors, such as the Ghysels, have accumulated a great number of these items.

These artefacts are often accompanied by precious documents: old photographs, drawings and prints illustrating the accounts of early explorers and, very occasionally, a film, such as the one that Baron Victor von Plessen made among the Dayak in Borneo in 1935.

The Ambiguity of a Belt: a Garment or a Piece of Finery?

There is very early evidence of the use of belts in the West. Admittedly, they are sometimes commonplace garments and sometimes opulent pieces of finery. In Western fashion, belts come and go; they may be worn under the breasts, around the waist or on the hips. In traditional societies, they are never perceived as fickle fashion items that last a season or two, but always as a functional and useful part of one's attire. Although belts are functional, they sometimes take on a special appearance due to the materials chosen to make them. Obviously, although the functional and decorative aspects are important, they do not fully account for the role that belts play. Sometimes they take on a symbolic significance, and sometimes they are politically and socially charged. They are also used in a number of rites. For many ethnic groups, tying and untying a belt is not a gratuitous act: unfastening a belt is a way of offering one's body to another person—that is, a body wrapped in a covering of fabric held in place by the belt. Hellenists, even more than African specialists, have written at length about the circumstances surrounding the baring of the body, which, in some circumstances can be frightening.[1]

Although it belongs to quite a different culture, the Japanese *obi* is also erotically charged. The relationship with the other, as an object of desire, is less clearly expressed in Africa. But does this mean it does not exist? It is more often concealed and kept strictly within the private sphere. When old Ogotemmêli told Marcel Griaule about the female genitals and their encounter with the male organ, he spoke in the metaphorical language that is used for myths and talked about the sex act without ever clearly naming it. Among the Winié in Burkina Faso, sex can be referred to only by allusion and innuendo. Yet it underlies all conversation and, at the slightest opportunity, is hinted at with knowing smiles and ambiguous gestures and metaphors.

On the other hand, belts can be part of the trappings used to assert sacred power, as in the Kuba Kingdom and related monarchies.

They may also mean a rise in the hierarchy, as in the *Bwami* graded societies among the Lega in the Congo, or be a symbol of social position—such as that of a wife or the mother of a male child, a status that is highly valued by the Ndebele people of South Africa, for instance. They sometimes have the power to protect the body of pregnant women as among the Luluwa in the Congo, or to increase fertility as among the Berbers in North Africa.

Of course, like all other kinds of jewellery, belts are part of a woman's dowry, indicating both the share of wealth that the bride brings to her in-laws and what she receives from her husband. The dowry remains at the woman's disposal for the whole of her life. In the steppes of Central Anatolia and the Caucasus, belts are a necessary item of clothing, but, when they are part of a set of finery, they also display their owners' wealth; they sometimes include materials or decorations that have prophylactic powers.

In India and Southeast Asia, belts are not purely functional either, as we must not forget that in Hindu philosophy beauty is a universal divine principle which ensures harmony in the world.

Certainly, belts have many functions, but it would be a pity not to emphasize the important role played by their accessories, especially in Asia. Everywhere, in all social classes, people attach all kinds of small items to their belts: chopstick holders, needle cases, purses of all sizes, fans, lighters, tobacco or betel nut pouches and protective amulets. In short, whatever they want to keep within easy reach!

Cache-sexe were as often worn by women as by men. Mangbetu women, in the Congo, added buttock aprons, too, while the Mongo used to wear fibre pompons in the small of their backs to accentuate the roundness of their buttocks. The Kirdi people of the Cameroons and Nigeria used a great variety of shapes and materials. When no other garment is worn, a *cache-sexe* protects a woman's sex organs which, like any other orifice, are particularly vulnerable to the intrusion of evil forces. That is why women seldom go completely naked, except in a few tribes such as the Nambikwara in the Mato Grosso region of Brazil. And very often, body painting, feathers and down give the illusion of covering their nakedness, as among the Kaiapo in Brazil. On the contrary, the private parts of the male body are covered only by their nudity. But this Adamitical nakedness does not mean a lack of any sense of decency. Thus, among the Papuans in New Guinea, the elders teach children from an early age not to stare at a woman's genitals and breasts.

This book on belts and *cache-sexe* is the latest addition to the series of works[2] on the remarkable Ghysels collection of rings, earrings, bracelets and necklaces. To the best of our knowledge, this is the first specific publication on this subject. Admittedly, most *cache-sexe* lack any great aesthetic value and, until very recently, were regarded as purely of ethnographic interest. But to relegate them all to such a status would be to overlook those that deserve to take their place alongside other items of traditional finery and play their role in beautifying the body.

[1] Guignard, Pascal, *Le sexe et l'ef-froi*, Gallimard, Paris, 1996

[2] van Cutsem, Anne, *A World of Rings: Africa, Asia and America, Skira*, Milan, 2000.

van Cutsem, Anne, *A World of Earrings: Africa, Asia and America*, Skira, Milan, 2001.

van Cutsem, Anne, *A World of Bracelets: Africa, Asia, Oceania and America*, Skira, Milan, 2002.

Leurquin, Anne, *A World of Necklaces: Africa, Asia, Oceania and America*, Skira, Milan, 2003.

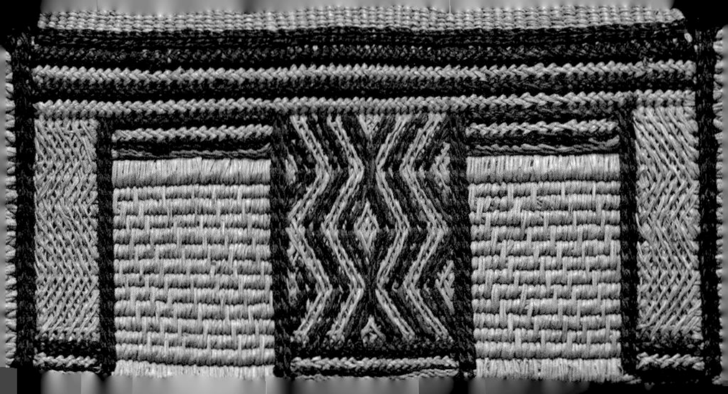

Africa

North Africa

The territories occupied by Morocco and Tunisia in North Africa have been historically and culturally conditioned by their geographical position, the first on the Atlantic seaboard and the second facing the Mediterranean. Despite differences between them, there are close affinities in their intensive use of weaving, including the belts that the Berber women make for themselves and their husbands.

The *fouta* is a long, broad strip of cloth wound several times around the waist and worn high on the torso like a corset. The men tuck into their belts the daggers known as *komia* with their finely chased silver scabbards. The belts of the Ait Ouaouzguite tribe are made of wool or silk; those worn by groups in the High Atlas Mountains are plaited and decorated with trinkets.

For all these tribes, red symbolizes the source of life and fertility. However, middle-class women in the imperial cities of Fez, Meknes, Rabat and Marrakech favoured broad, long brocade belts that were tied at the side and decorated with different patterns and colours to go with their clothing. (p. 15).

In the Tafilalet region of southeast Morocco, at traditional Jewish weddings between children who had barely reached puberty, the boy would wear a similar belt, woven from gold and silver threads in the workshops of Fez. Another type of belt, narrower and woven or embroidered with silk, was fastened with a buckle made of chased silver or, more rarely, of gold. (pp. 16–7).

In the 1930s Jean Besancenot noted that this fine craftwork had all but disappeared, although Jewish goldsmiths were still active at the time.[1]

West and Equatorial Africa

For many centuries, the *cache-sexe* was the only article of clothing worn by most ethnic groups in West Africa. But there was not necessarily anything particularly original in its design that would interest us today. In most cases it disappeared under another garment such as the skirt worn by Dogon women. However, Marcel Griaule's interviews with Ogotemmêli reveal its importance in the sex life of Dogon couples.[2]

The Kirdi and related groups living in the grasslands of the Cameroons possess the most impressive assortment of these garments. The name *Kirdi*, meaning pagan, was given to them by the Muslim Fulbe, who threatened to enslave them. All these groups fled to the mountainous area of the Mandara. The *cache-sexe* is their only garment and is made of a wide variety of materials. Before the introduction of Islam, at the end of the eighteenth century, the *Fon*, or kings, and dignitaries in the royal courts, especially the Bamum court, also wore them, as can be seen on royal statues. However, several *Fon* were converted to Islam, which regarded *cache-sexe* as indecent and so at odds with the demands of royal dignity. Kirdi *cache-sexe* make great use of coloured glass beads (pp. 30–1) and cowries with fine twisted leather laces (p. 46); they are occasionally decorated with beetle carapaces. Other, smaller versions are made of fine strips of iron fashioned into the form of a shell (p. 45). Some had little bells that tinkled when the wearer danced or walked along in order to frighten off evil spirits.

Central Africa: the Kuba and Mangbetu Kingdoms

The Kuba preferred belts: the sacred nature of royal power required paraphernalia including belts because they held in place the 'pagne', consisting of many layers of cloth, which the king wore around his waist. Sometimes several belts were required, depending on the type of garment worn by the king, the princes or the dignitaries. The king wore several, one over another; they were made of large numbers of cowry shells sewn to a strip of woven plant fibres (pp. 80–1). The belts and the rest of his finery sometimes weighed over eighty kilograms! The centrepiece is a specific knot made of beads called a *woot* after the tribe's founder. The knot symbolizes power and is an omnipresent motif because it is also found on fabrics and in scar patterns on the skin of high-ranking women (p. 83).

The Mangbetu kingdom in north-eastern Congo was at the height of its power in the second half of the nineteenth century. Until very recently, the king and the noble class had anatomical deformities such as misshapen skulls. The body painting once used by the men and high-ranking women, as may be seen on statues from this area, now seems to be limited to women. The latter used to wear a *cache-sexe* made of banana leaves, flattened, dried and sewn together, and decorated with a cylinder in front (p. 67), while a *negbe*, or buttock apron, of the same material, decorated with a geometrical pattern, was attached to the belt at the back (pp. 64–5). Among the Ekonda, a Mongo subgroup, a pompon of plant fibres was worn in the small of the back to emphasize the curve of the spine.

Mangbetu men used to wear a broad belt of twisted, polished vines around their waists, holding an apron of beaten bark, either plain or with a two-tone pattern.[3]

Not far away, the Mbuti pygmies, who live in the Ituri Forest, are renowned for their beaten bark *cache-sexe* decorated with stripes, spirals and arabesques that pay no heed to symmetry. The patterns are thought to have its origins in body painting.[4] This original decoration conjures up Paul Klee's use of poetic signs (p. 74).[5]

In traditional cultures, the male sex organ is said to be 'closed' and the female organ 'open'. Françoise Héritier believes that 'this differential power' establishes the difference between the sexes, with its many consequences.[6] One of these consequences is the vulnerability of the female genitals, which are constantly threatened by the intrusion of evil spirits, causing, for instance, sterility and miscarriages. They must, therefore, be more carefully protected than the male organs, so that all societies made artefacts to ward off the danger inherent in the female sex organs. This is why, from the second month of pregnancy, Luluwa women donned a leather belt decorated with ivory balls and beads or cowries filled with magic substances. This belt and the *cache-sexe mubangu* were worn until the baby was born. Few of these garments have survived, but they appear on a number of statues.[7] The same custom is found in some aboriginal communities in India, such as the Abor and the Gallong.

Conversely, in the *Bwami* secret society among the Lega in the Congo, women who have reached menopause may compete with men for the highest rank. The sign that they have attained the same social position as the men is the right to wear a belt of coloured beads, to which a small ivory phallus is attached; the belt also holds up a red beaten bark apron (p. 75).

East and South Africa

East Africa has been populated for thousands of years by herdsmen whose main concern is protecting their pastures and access to the wells they need to water their huge herds. The Masai and Turkana in Kenya and the Cuanhama, Himba and Huila in Namibia, have a social structure based on a hierarchy of age groups including both sexes. During the initiation ceremonies that mark the passage from one state to another, finery serves as a clearly identifiable visual code. Young Turkana women wear belts of ostrich eggshell beads sewn on a leather strap, along with another smaller belt made of coloured glass beads; the two together proclaim their marital status. Young Cuanhama men give their fiancées *omakipa,* which are ivory buttons carved with abstract patterns and sewn on a strip of leather hung on a belt (p. 89). Their number reflects the size of the young man's herd and his interest in his future wife. Very often, Himba (p. 87) or Samburu belts made of iron beads, like the *omakipa,* are covered with a patina of the grease the women use to keep their skin smooth and ward off insects.

The Bushmen of the Kalahari desert, who belong to the ancient San group, had fewer materials at their disposal, so they made their *cache-sexe* from bone beads threaded on plant fibres or from ostrich eggshell beads (pp. 90–1).

Before European colonisation, South Africa was occupied by various ethnic groups, some of which, like the Zulus, were organized in kingdoms. In 1848, the Zulu king, Mpande, opened up his territory to foreign merchants, who were astonished to find such an abundance of wealth.

They noticed that the king wore a belt of blue and green glass beads; these unusual beads probably came from China or India, brought through South African ports by Arab traders. The Europeans quickly grasped the value of the trade in glass beads: they were export-ed in bulk and helped develop the beadwork attributed to both the Zulus and the Nguni.

The size of the belt worn with the *cache-sexe* and the coloured patterns that decorated it not only pro-claimed the woman's status but functioned as a system of communication, as the patterns conveyed several meanings. The example of Ndebele beadwork testifies to the excellence achieved in this type of craftwork, which points to the existence of a much earlier tradition of which nothing has survived. Each step in a woman's life requires special beadwork: the plain *ligabi* belt is for girls; when they reach puberty, they exchange it for another, the *isiphephethu*. Next comes the two-piece *lipotho* apron and lastly the five-piece *ijogolo*, which a woman gives her daughter-in-law when she considers her worthy of her son (p. 103).[8]

[1] Besancenot, J., *Costumes du Maroc*, La Croisée des Chemins/Édisud, Aix en Provence, 1939; reprint 2000, pp. 142–3.
[2] Griaule, M., *Dieu d'eau, entretiens avec Ogotommêli*, Fayard, Paris, 1966, p. 75.
[3] Bastin, M.L., *Introduction aux Arts d'Afrique noire,* Arts d'Afrique Noire, Arnouville, 1984, p. 376. See also: Burssens, H, *Mangbetu, Art de cour africain de collections privées belges*, exhibition catalogue, Kredietbank, Brussels, 1992, for painted statues of both males and females.
[4] Ibid., p. 28, ill. 12.
[5] Coquet, M., *Textiles africains*, Adam Biro, Paris, 1998, pp. 122–3.
[6] Héritier, F., *Masculin/Féminin. La pensée de la différence*, Odile Jacob, Paris, 1996.
[7] *Trésors d'Afrique. Musée de Tervuren*, ed. G. Verswijver et al., exhibition catalogue, Musée royal de l'Afrique centrale, Tervuren, 1995, pp. 134–5.
[8] Ghysels, E., *La parure perlée chez les Ndebele*, degree dissertation, Université Libre de Bruxelles, 1986–87. See also: *ubuntu, Arts et Cultures d'Afrique du Sud*, Musée national des Arts d'Afrique et d'Océanie, Paris, Réunion des musées nationaux, Paris, 2002, pp. 341–2.

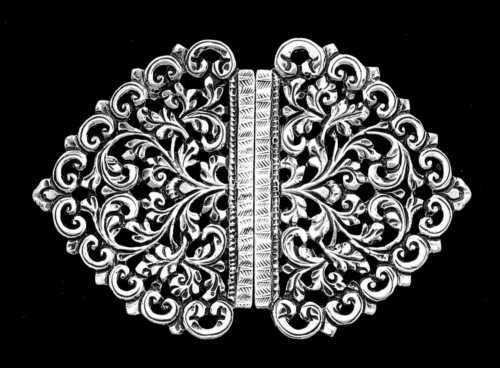

24

25

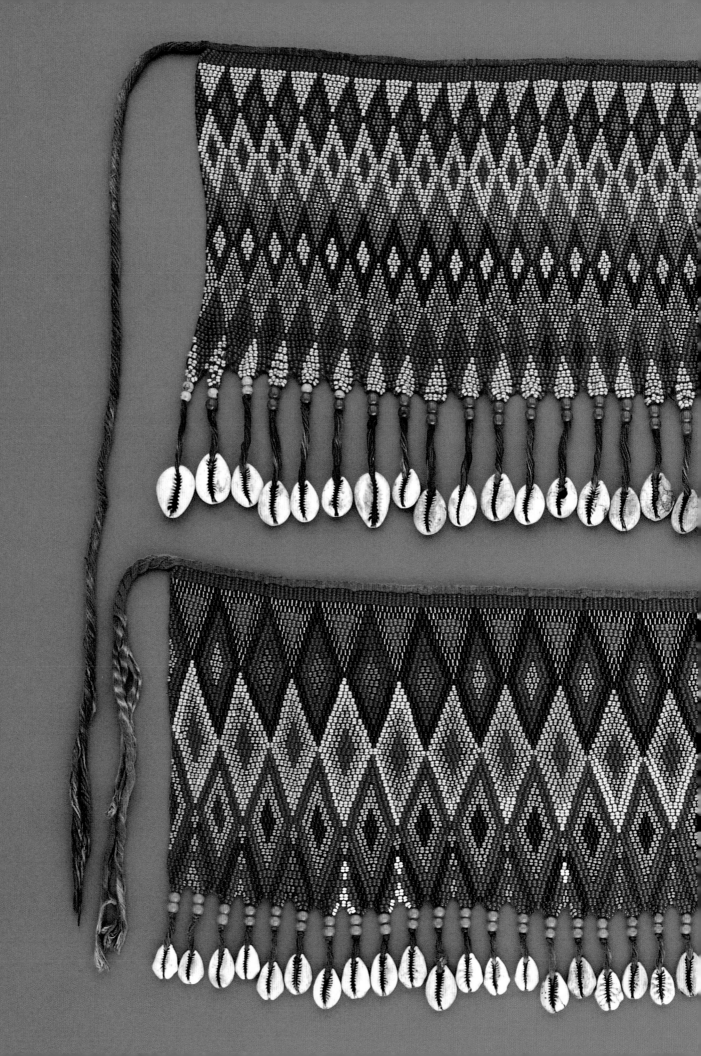

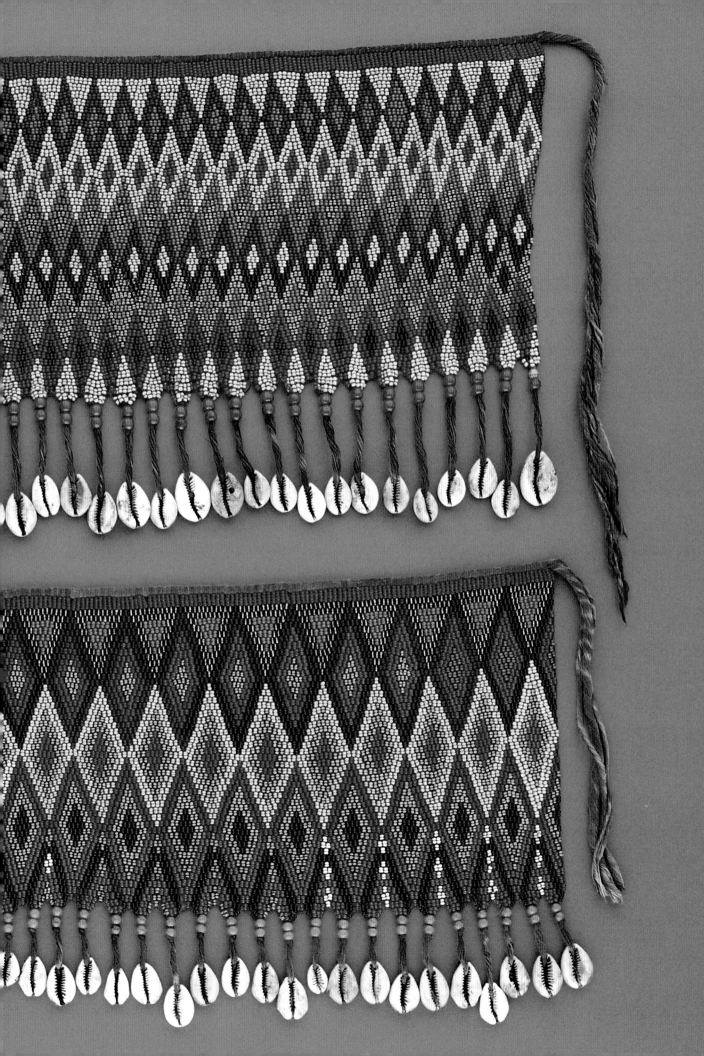

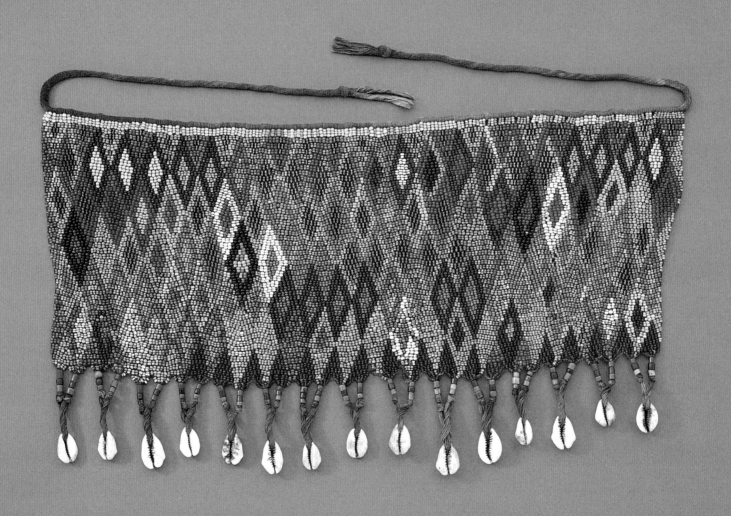

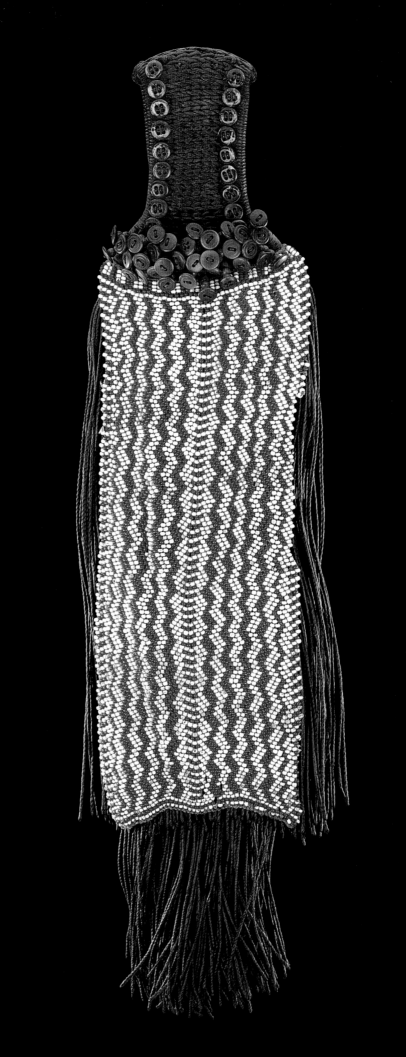

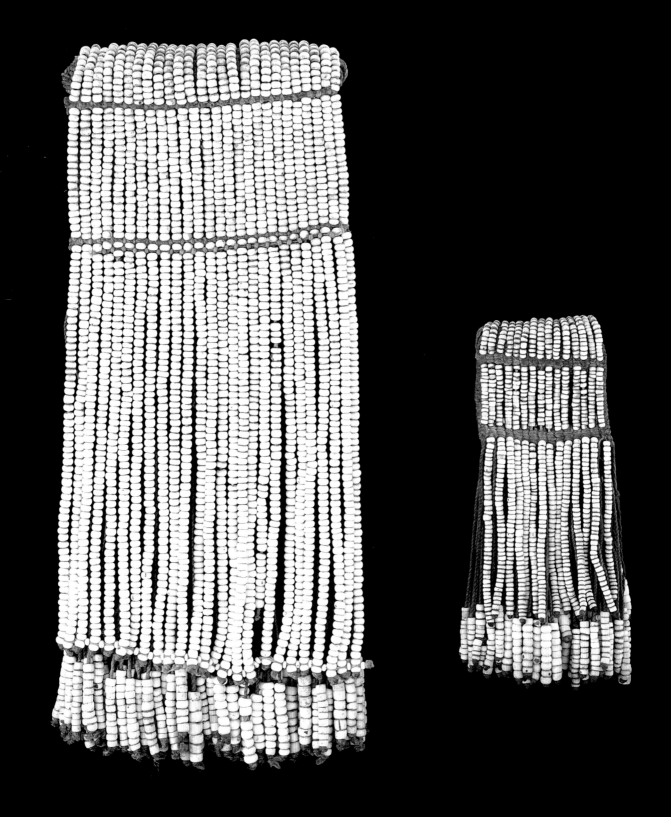

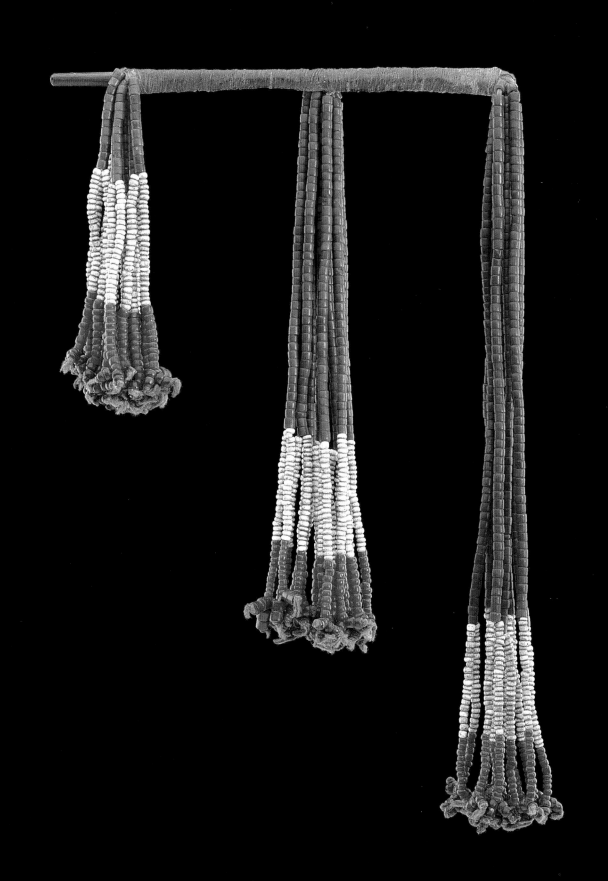

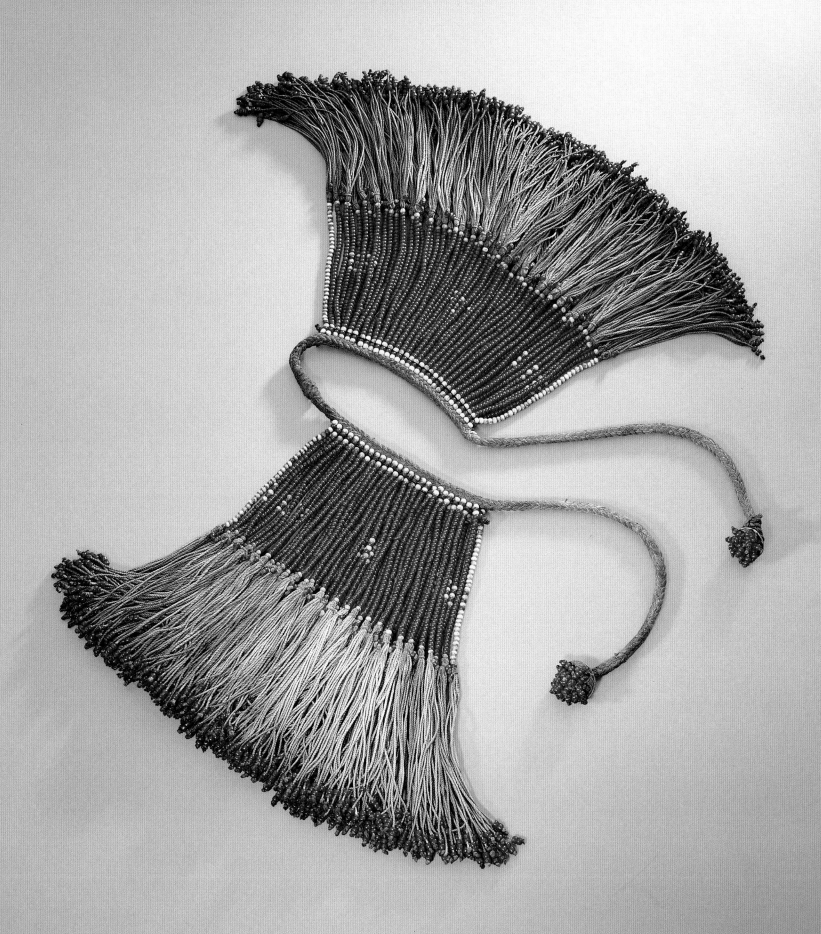

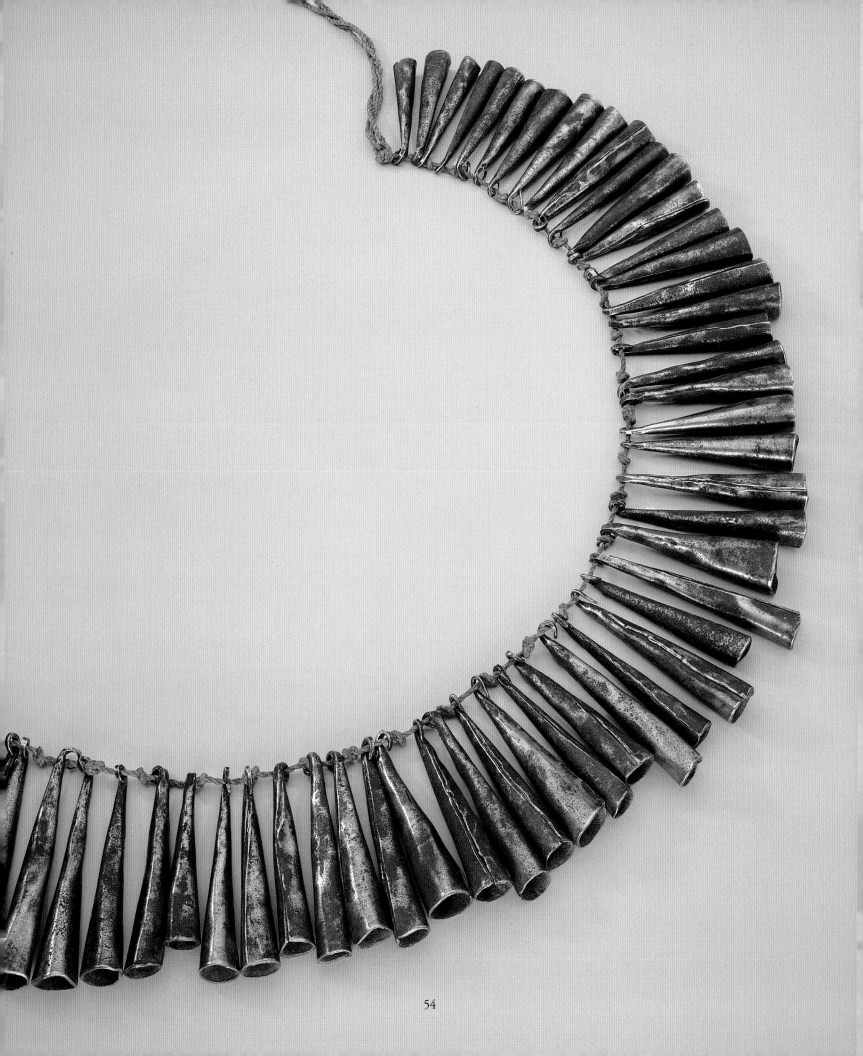

58

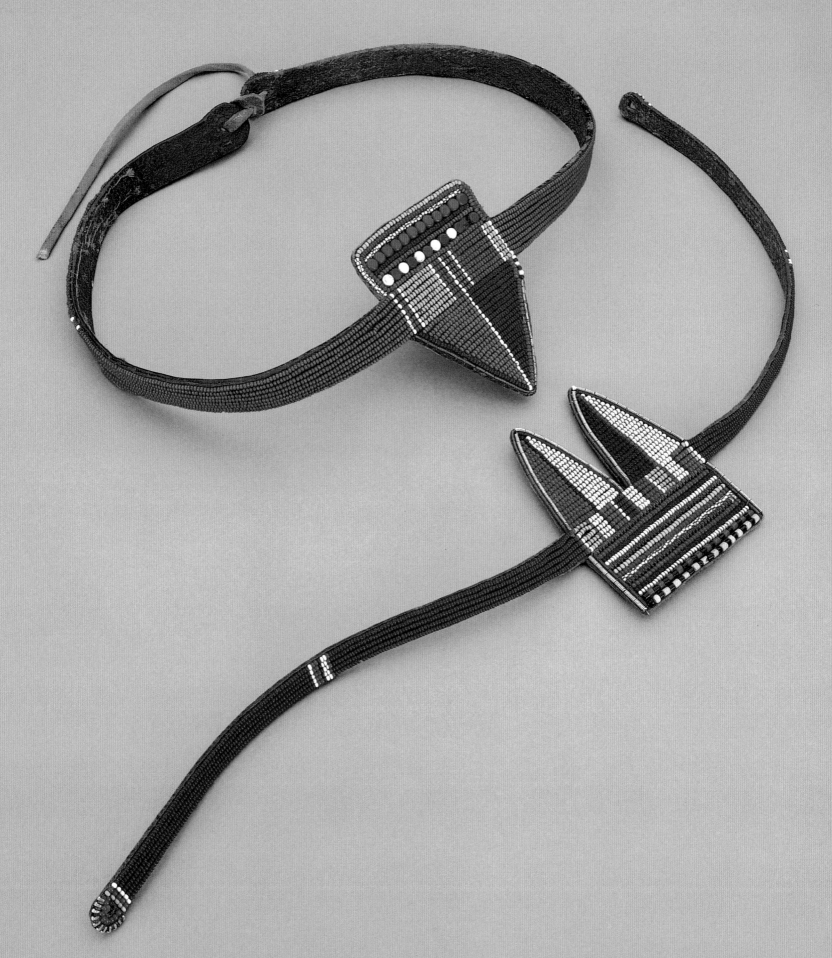

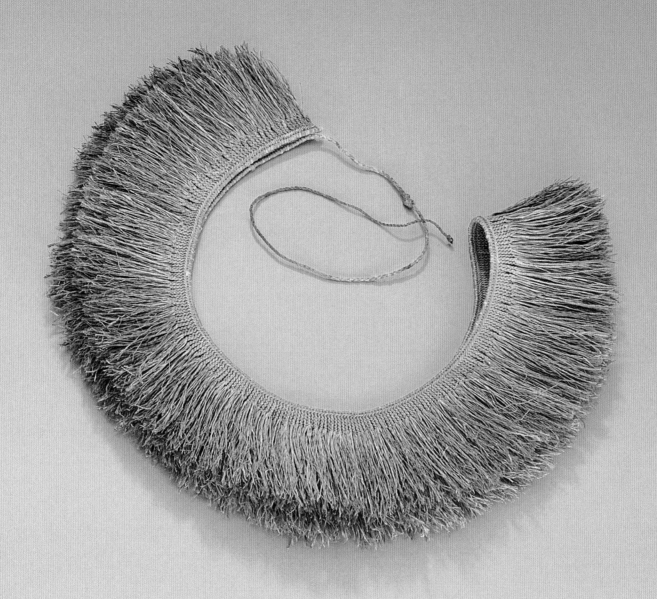

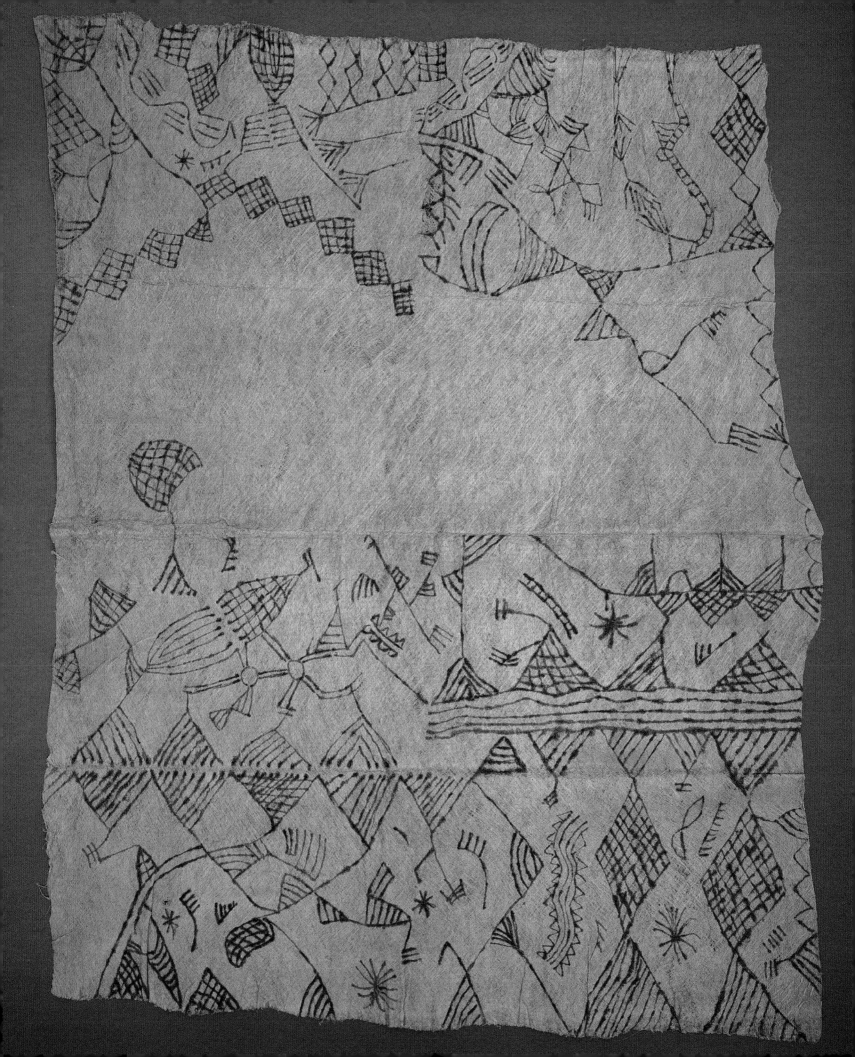

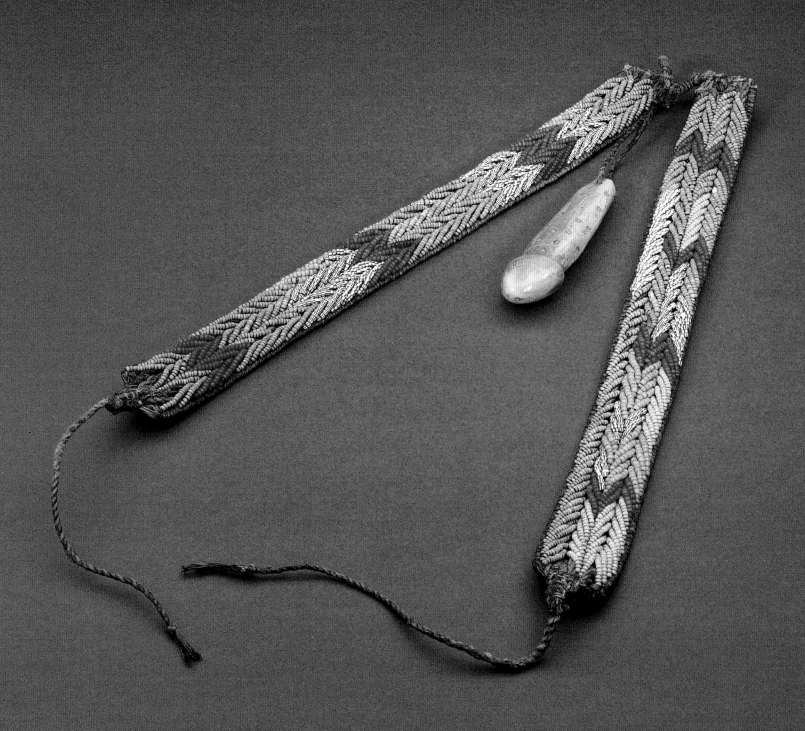

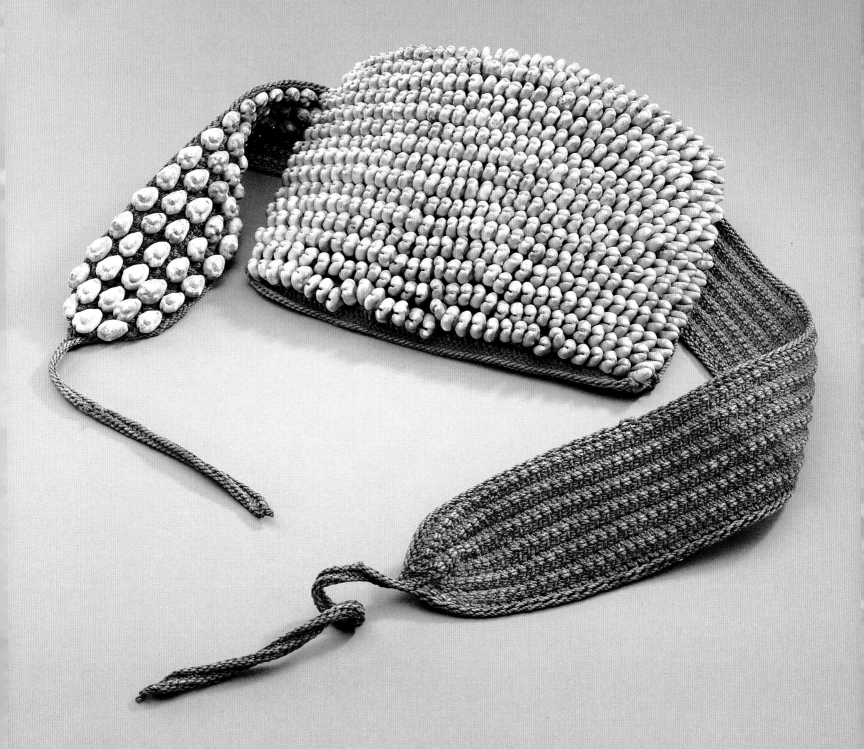

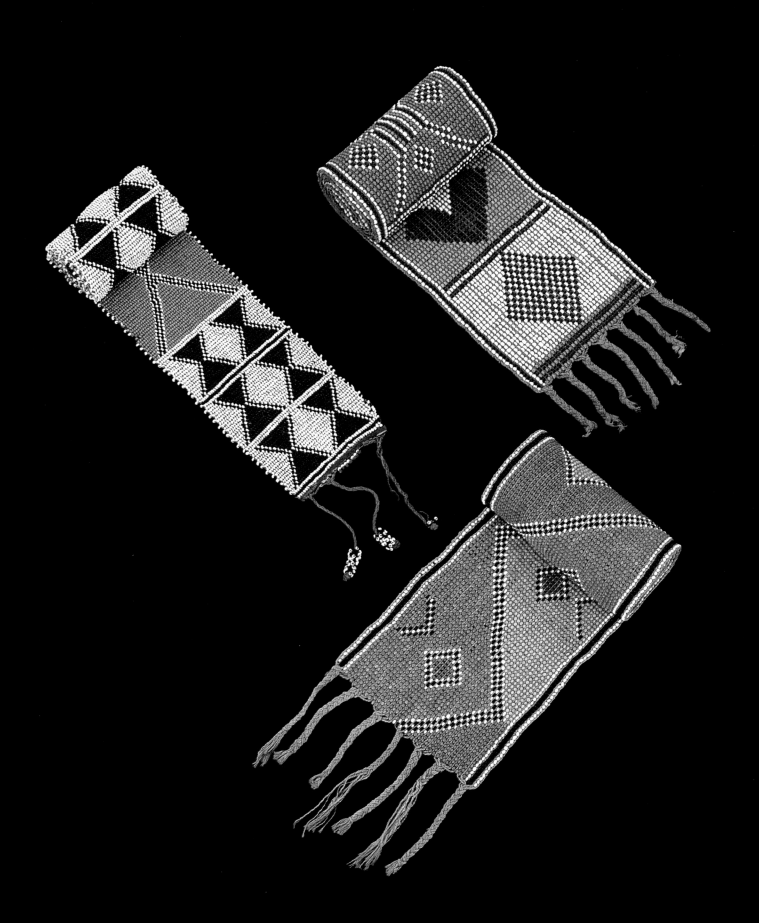

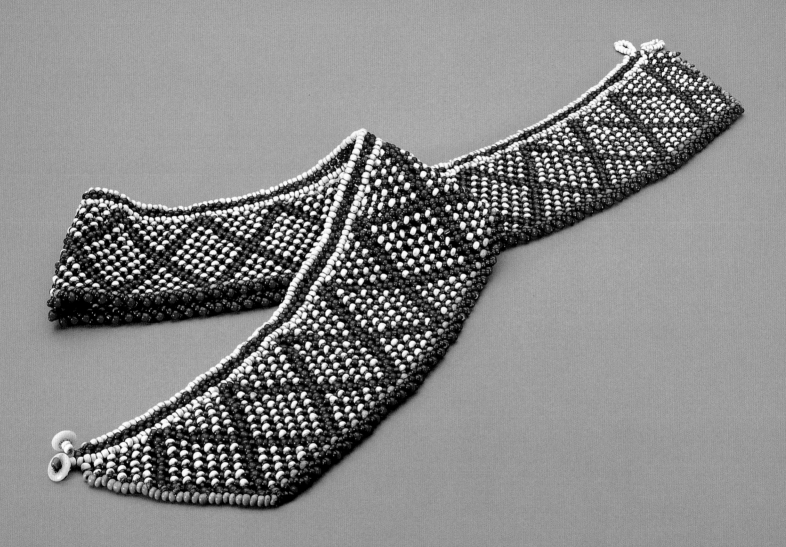

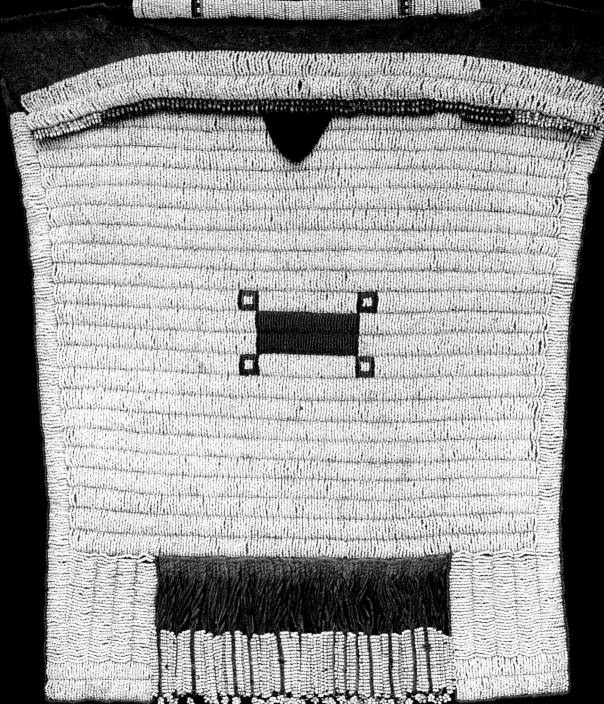

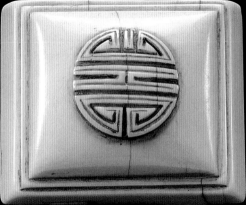

Asia

The Arabian Peninsula: Yemen and the Sultanate of Oman

Located at the southern end the Arabian Peninsula, Yemen and the Sultanate of Oman share the same economic and cultural history. They both accepted Islam—which explains the lack of *cache-sexe*—and they both engaged in trade, Yemen for incense and other balsamic substances, the Sultanate of Oman for exotic wood from India and China.[1]

The belts worn by Yemenite women, like their other finery, display the wealth of the merchant class. Made by Jewish goldsmiths (p. 115), they are worn at the wedding ceremony and during the first year of marriage.

Jewish goldsmiths are highly skilled in various techniques such as granulation and filigree work, with ornamental effects. They also inset coral or coloured glass beads. The men wear leather belts, sometimes covered with brocade, to which they add richly decorated money pouches or leather purses decorated with cornelian cabochons. The dagger known as a *jambiya*, the ultimate male attribute, is also tucked into the belt.

In Oman, the women wear similar belts, decorated with numerous chains, in 'rat's tails' or with medallions. The men's belts are also adorned with leather purses or hold their favourite weapon, a curved dagger, similar to the Yemenite *jambiya*. As in other Islamic countries, belts and other pieces of finery indicate the wearer's wealth and social status.

Turkey, The Caucasus, Central Asia

In Turkey, belt buckles are sometimes decorated with enamel or carved coral cabochons, (pp. 118–9); coral is believed to have prophylactic powers in Turkey while agates are prized for the same reason in the Caucasus.

Located between the Black Sea and the Caspian Sea, the Caucasus is now made up of the federated republics of Armenia, Azerbaijan and Georgia, as well as Dages-

tan, whereas Turkmenistan, further east, borders on the Eurasian steppes. Caucasian belts often combine strips of brocade or leather with silver or silver-gilt buckles or clasps (pp. 124–5). According to ancient beliefs inherited from ancestral shamanism, the gleaming silver represents water and fire. The tunic, which is the traditional male garment worn by the nomads roaming the steppes, requires silver or leather belts decorated with chased silver ornaments to hold, depending on the wearer's wealth, a dagger, finely carved silver boxes or humble leather pouches. Georgian and Armenian goldsmiths are famed for their metalwork: their craftsmanship is particularly in evidence on the more sophisticated women's belts, with chasing and niello to heighten the design. The use of niello and inset coloured stones or glass beads is particularly characteristic of buckles from Dagestan. In Azerbaijan, a miniature dagger imitating the real weapon (p. 128) is thrust through the two parts of the buckle. Wider and more ornate men's belts come from the Bukhara region in Uzbekistan (p. 129). They were particularly appreciated by the ancient Khans, nomadic chieftains, such as Genghis Khan. Jewellers also make them in finely worked silver or silver gilt, sometimes decorated with cloisonné enamel in delicate colours, mosaics of turquoises or cabochons of red and green glass beads, the colours of Islam.

Already adopted by goldsmiths in antiquity, niello is a technique in which a dark composition of metallic alloys is used to inlay engraved designs, which, in this piece, are arabesques resembling Arabic calligraphy (p. 123).

In these ancient nomadic lands, where horses and riders as swift as the wind are worshipped, there is evidently no place for a *cache-sexe*.

India

Part of all marriage arrangements in rural communities in India, the dowry, *stridhana,* requires a large amount of jewellery. More than for the number of pieces, this is appreciated for its weight, which must be commensurate with the status and demands of the husband's family. Belts have a significant place in this finery.

Not merely a display of wealth, belts and jewellery protect the body from harm. This talismanic aspect, which is derived from residual animistic beliefs, is accepted in certain Buddhist and Hindu sects, and rural Indian jewellery probably owes its longevity to its magical and religious function. Rural communities, especially in the north, have always preferred silver, whereas gold is favoured in the cities and in the south. It is, however, surprising to see such quantities of silver jewellery because India has few silver deposits.[2] The demand was such that from Roman times onwards—as early as the first century AD, in fact—it stimulated trade in rare materials such as silk and precious woods in exchange for silver coins. Moreover, jewellery that did not accompany the dead could be hoarded or melted down and reused in a perpetual cycle, a well-known theme in Hindu philosophy. Different manufacturing techniques produce different effects. Rather than by ethnic group or region, Oppi Untracht groups the belts by form—rigid, supple or meshed—and lists major stylistic variations within each group.[3] Most are made of silver, but the models vary widely (pp. 148–9). They are covered with figures, sometimes alluding to the *Ramayana* epic with its famous divine heroes. The *Kama Sutra* is another source of imagery and Hindu beliefs contribute elements such as the cone-shaped buckled representing the holy mountain, Mount Meru.

The *cache-sexe* puts in a brief appearance in India: silver *yoni* shapes are used to cover the genitals of children, especially little girls. *Cache-sexe* and nudity go well together in a hot climate!

The Naga have a *cache-sexe* in the form of an apron covered with cowries and a brass disc (p. 158). In the Andaman Islands—where, however, it is seldom worn—it takes the shape of a small net apron, threaded with fine shells (p. 161).

In India, finery and nudity are part of the notion of beauty that generates desire and self-fulfilment. Sculptures decked with jewellery, including sumptuous belts, express the birth of the universe engendered by primordial copulation. This violent sensuality is reserved for the gods. But there is no shame in the body and its needs: the statues in explicit erotic positions in the temples disturb the worshippers less than they do Western visitors, although, in reality, Indian women are very prudish. They swathe themselves in their saris from head to foot, leaving only a glimpse of their navels, and this garment makes them inaccessible. In the same way, the nakedness of antique Greek statues was unrelated to the way people dressed; at that time, in fact, women were required to wear a heavy woollen peplos, drawn in at the waist.

The Himalayas: Tibet

Himalayan jewellery fulfils several functions. It defines social status, is associated with political and religious power and has a talismanic role, initially linked to popular Buddhist and Hindu beliefs. Belts may be made of cloth, leather, bronze or silver, but are seldom made of gold, a precious metal reserved for the upper spheres of political and religious power (p. 170). Regarded as having prophylactic properties, turquoises are often used in belts, especially by the women of Lhasa. On ceremonial occasions and in their everyday lives they wear a half-belt with a hook at each end to hold the apron which shows that they are married (pp. 164–5).

These ornaments may be made of silver embellished with gold and turquoise insets, or of bronze. Members of the civil service hang a seal and a box of red wax on their belts (p. 167). The belts of both men and women are cluttered with all manner of objects, but the women's chatelaine is the most spectacular of all. Hooked on to the belt or bodice, it has a mass of little chains holding all those little necessities that they cannot find another place for, such as tweezers and ear cleaners. In Ladakh, a region of eastern Kashmir in north-western India, belts are hung with an ornament composed of cowries and a large medallion engraved with a continuous knot pattern, a symbol of love and eternity.

Mongolia, China, Japan

Mongolian belts are worn by men and women alike. They are made of fabric wound around the waist, or sometimes of leather decorated with silver. A sheath containing a knife and a pair of ivory chopsticks, a pipe in its case, or other small utilitarian objects are hung from them.

A lighter with an iron blade in a leather purse containing tow and flints, decorated with patterns inspired by the Chinese floral repertoire, or by the animals represented in the art of the steppes, completes the set. These curious objects, which characterize Mongolian as much as Tibetan culture, are held in place by counterweights inserted in the belt and attached to each item by a small chain (pp. 198–9). Some of them show remarkable craftsmanship and skill in combining diverse techniques.

In China, it is not unusual for other items, such as snuff pouches, needle-holders and spectacle cases, to be hooked onto the belt by means of a toggle (pp. 180–1), a charming, protective object made of ivory or wood, which is a forerunner of the Japanese *netsuke*. The latter, made to hold an *inro*, a finely decorated medicine box usually made of lacquered wood, are often made by famous artists and are sometimes signed (pp. 202–3).

Southeast Asia

Forming part of the countries grouped under the generic term of Southeast Asia, Myanmar (formerly Burma), Thailand, Laos, Vietnam and Cambodia were gradually conquered by people from southern China. Archaeological excavations confirm a shared historical background which is still perceptible despite the strong cultural hybridization due to the co-existence of a large number of ethnic groups over thousands of years. The cultural mix was fostered by trade with South India and the Malay Archipelago from the first millennium onwards: the birth of the first Indianized states was one of the consequences of this ocean trade. The spread of Buddhism and Hinduism, and later Islam in Indonesia, changed the living conditions of the traditional societies; despised by their rulers, they fled to the northern boundaries of these territories where they still survive today. Finery in Southeast Asia can be divided into two categories: refined pieces that are part of a long tradition of jewellery-making directly descended from the historical dynasties; and the jewellery of the ethnic minorities which is of a completely different nature. While it is true that their jewellery uses metal, precious or otherwise, enamel and inset stones, these belts have special functions that are not strictly limited to the display of ostentatious wealth.

In northern Myanmar, the chatelaine and its array of tiny utilitarian objects probably came originally from China, along with the enamelling technique sometimes used by the Shan jewellers to decorate the centre of the belt.

Thai and Cambodian belts are made of silver; the sophisticated techniques used to make and decorate them testify to the expertise handed down from one generation to another. The goldsmiths' skill in chasing, granulation and filigree work, as well as incised patterns, can be seen on the clasps. They represent birds, plants and sometimes the signs of the zodiac. The decorative cone in the centre of the clasp, which, as we have seen, represents the sacred mountain Mount Meru in the Hindu and Buddhist religions, symbolizes the axis of the world, the link between the gods and man. In the ninth century, at Angkor Vat in Cambodia, the statues of the sacred Apsara dancers were adorned with sumptuous belts, which give an idea of the excellence of Khmer craftsmanship.

Malay Archipelago

In particular, a great variety of belts may be found in the Philippines, where two islands produce large quantities of jewellery: island of Luzon, in the north, and Mindanao, in the south. Discovered in the northern part of Mindanao, the royal treasure of Surigao, dating from the seventh to the thirteenth centuries, contained a set of superb gold belts with a fine mesh of outstanding quality. The aristocratic Ifugao class, whose wealth was derived from rice production, were fond of wearing large amounts of jewellery. Worn over brightly coloured woven costumes, the belts enhanced the prestige of the ruling classes. The girls included them in the exchange of jewellery that was part of local marriage customs. In Mindanao, the Bagobo nobles wore large-meshed bronze belts to which they attached little bells on chains that tinkled when they danced (p. 212). The acquisition of a *sangilot,* when a Bagobo woman attained a high rank in a graded society, resembles the belts obtained by Lega women in a similar secret society in the Congo. Bontoc head hunters were presented with the *tikam,* a mother-of-pearl disk attached to the centre of the bronze chain they wore around their waists as a reward for their prowess (p. 213), as was the *upud,* a serrated shell disk decorated with a fine pattern in tortoiseshell or coconut shell (p. 219), which ensured great prestige.[4] This ornament is reminiscent of the *kap kap* found in New Ireland.

There are many common stylistic features in the belts of Sulawesi and Kalimantan, where, like other finery, they are used to celebrate the exploits of hunters and warriors. The intricacy of the gold finery from Sumatra is due to a dual iconographic tradition, derived partly from Hinduism and Buddhism, and partly from Islamic goldsmiths, who also contributed the technique of enamelling,[5] which was characteristic of jewellery from the ancient kingdom of Aceh. In the fifteenth century, the new capital Palembang welcomed many Chinese goldsmiths who brought their know-how with them. Sumatra, and nearby Malaysia, produced fabric belts with superb chased silver or gold clasps, sometimes nielloed, or made of copper inlaid with silver (p. 224). Rich finery was required for royal ceremonies, including gold belts worn over brocade or batik sarongs. The nobles also wore the kris, or sacred dagger, as fearsome for its magical and religious powers as for its razor-sharp blade. On the other hand, the belts worn by Iban Dayak women in Sarawak were tied tightly around the torso from waist to breasts. It functions as a small corset, like those worn by Balinese dancing girls, but here it is made of cane, decorated with bronze rings and fastened by a metal pin, or made in a single piece (pp. 232–3). Similar ornaments are found in the Moluccas (pp. 238–9).

In Sulawesi, many princely states in the coastal regions were once prosperous trading powers where social success was measured by the acquisition of gold jewellery. While they appreciated gold as a sign of wealth, the tribes in the interior, such as the Toraja, believed that it had supernatural powers as well. In Sumba and Flores, as in Nias and among the Batak people in Sumatra, the accumulation of prestigious objects and jewellery, including belts, stimulated the rivalry between the great families.

[1] *Ethnic Jewellery,* ed. John Mack, British Museum Press, London, 1994, p. 47 ff.
[2] Untracht, O., *Traditional Jewelry of India,* Thames and Hudson, London, 1997, Chap. 1.
[3] Ibid., p. 241 ff.
[4] Rodgers S., *L'or des îles. Bijoux et ornements d'Indonésie, de Malaisie, et des Philippines dans les Collections du Musée Barbier-Mueller,* Geneva, 1991, p. 339.
Eng. Ed.: *Power and Gold: Jewellery from Indonesia, Malaysia and the Philippines from the Barbier-Müller Collection, Geneva,* Prestel Publishing Ltd., London, 1988.
[5] Richter, A., *The Jewelry of Southeast Asia,* Thames & Hudson Ltd., London, 2000, p. 155.

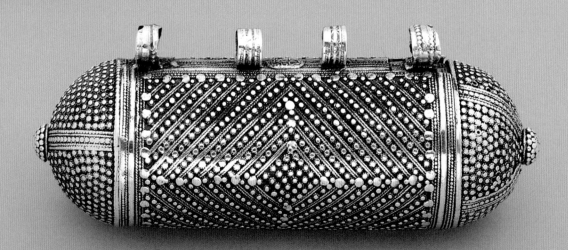

114

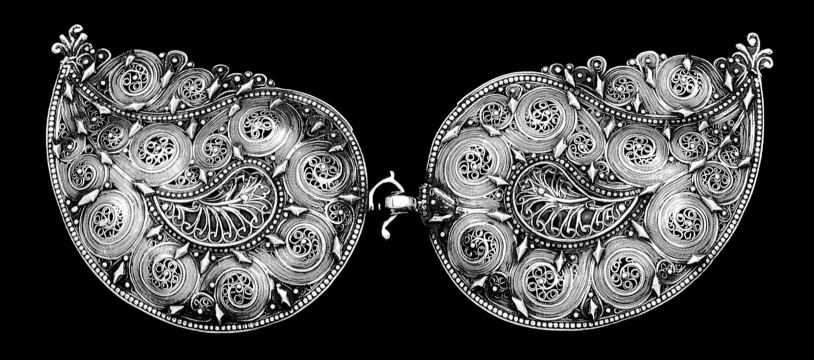

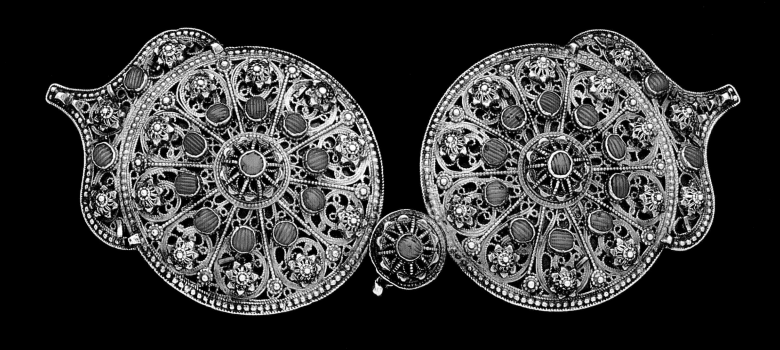

120

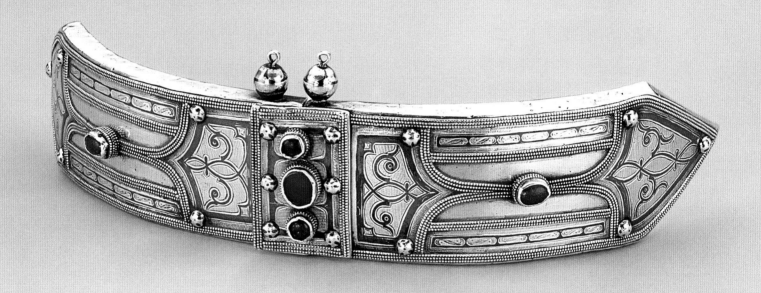

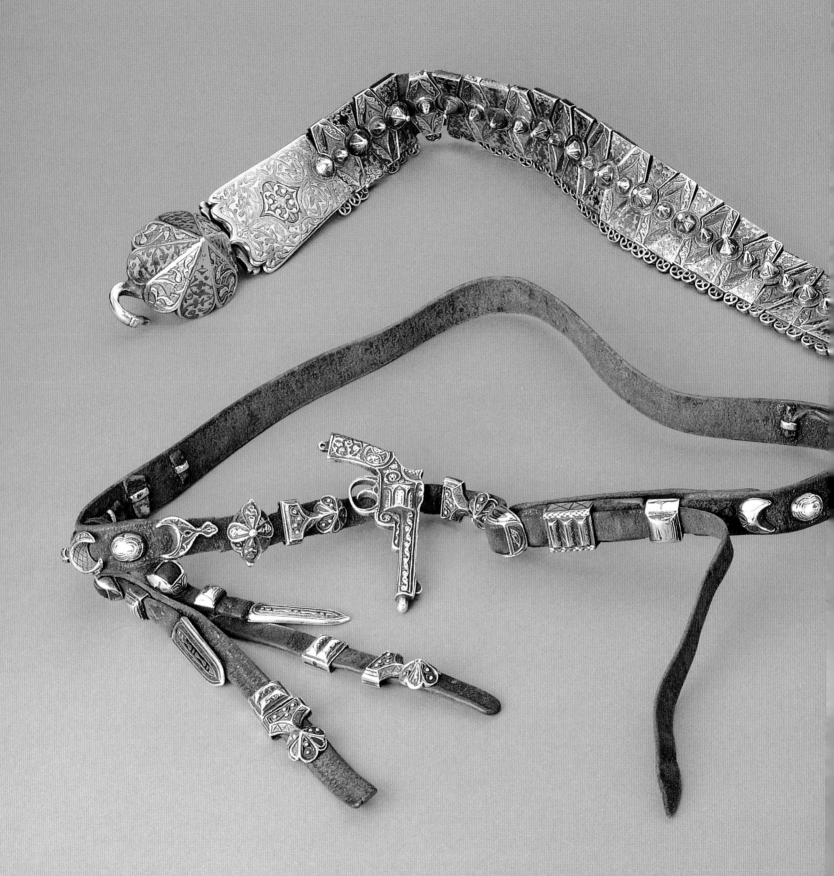

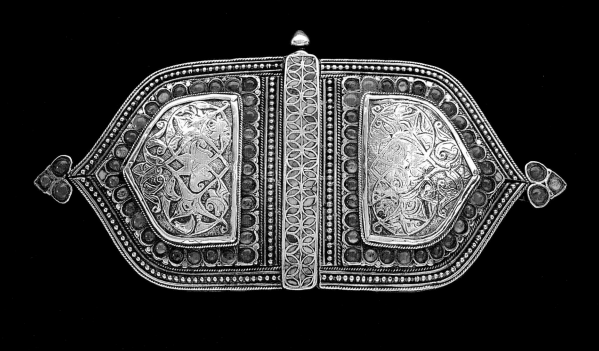

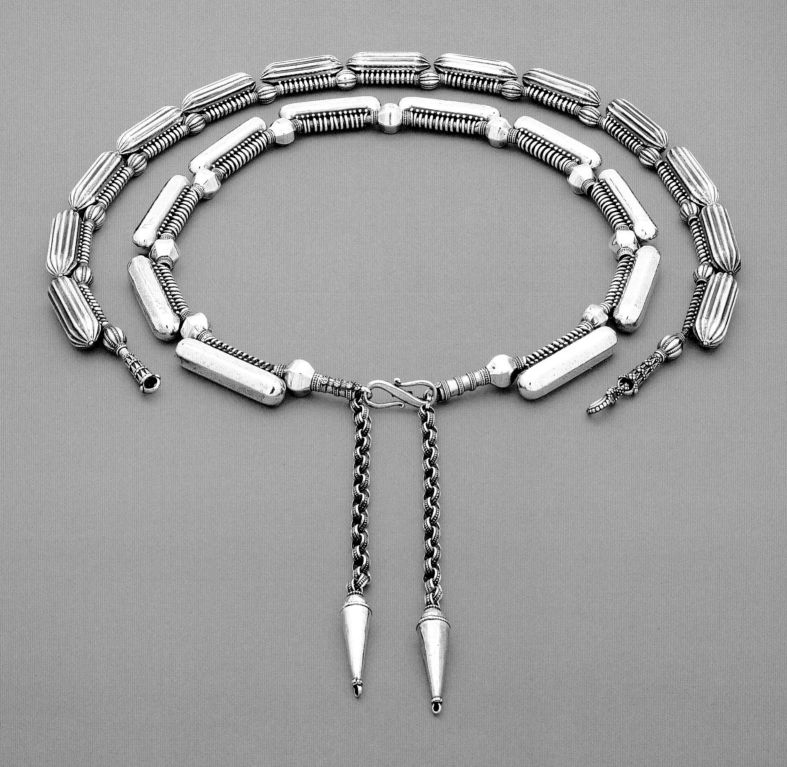

138

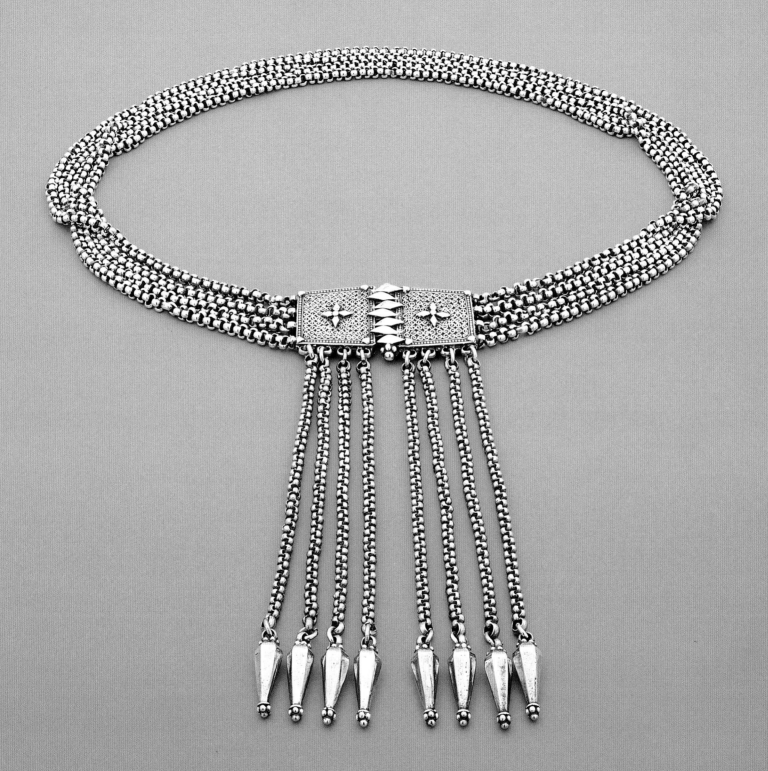

140

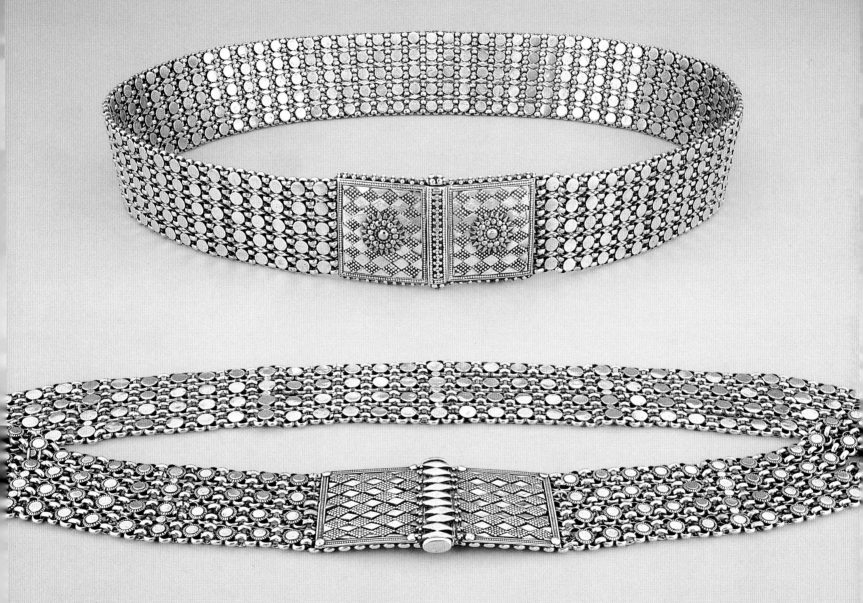

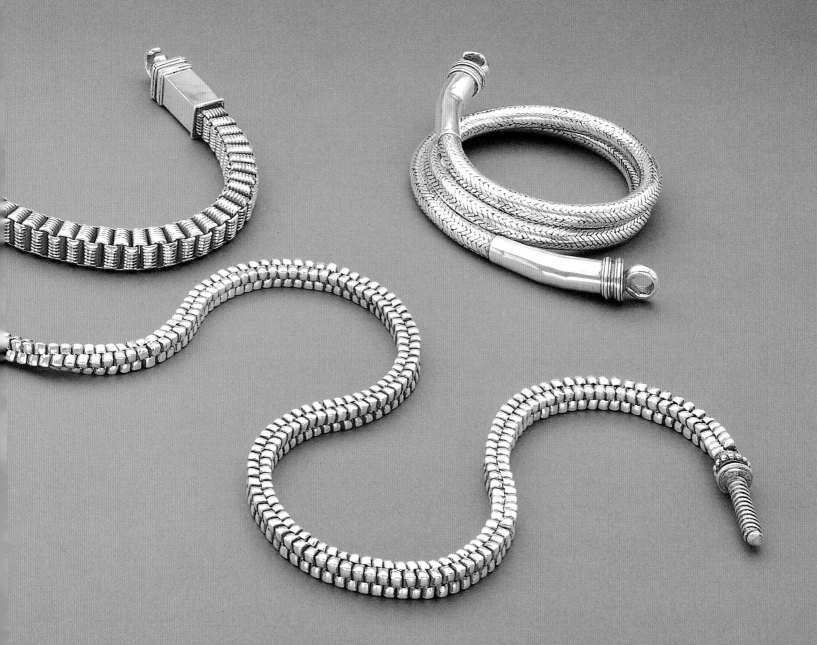

143

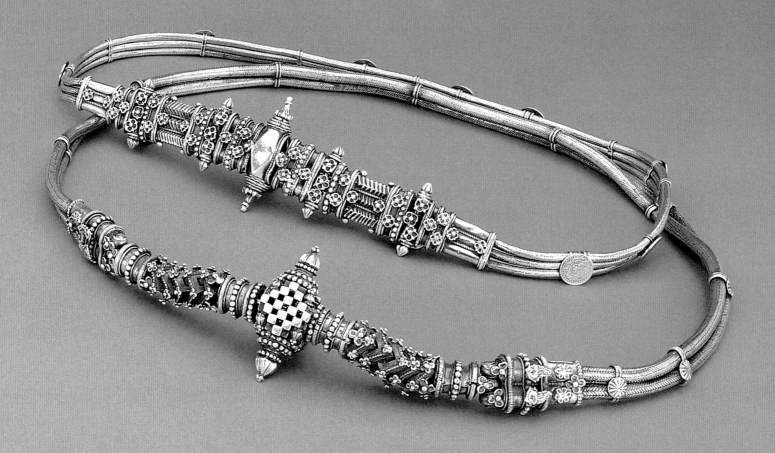

149

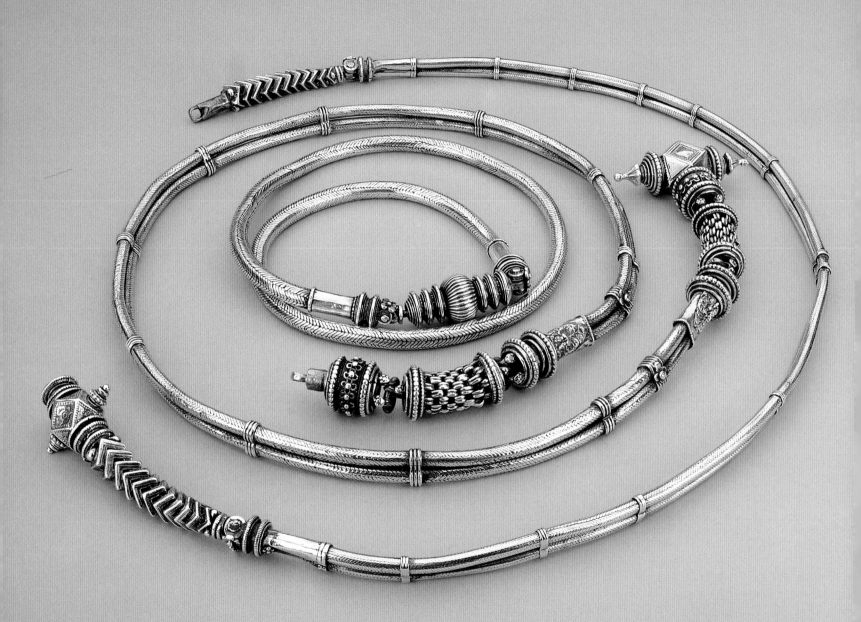

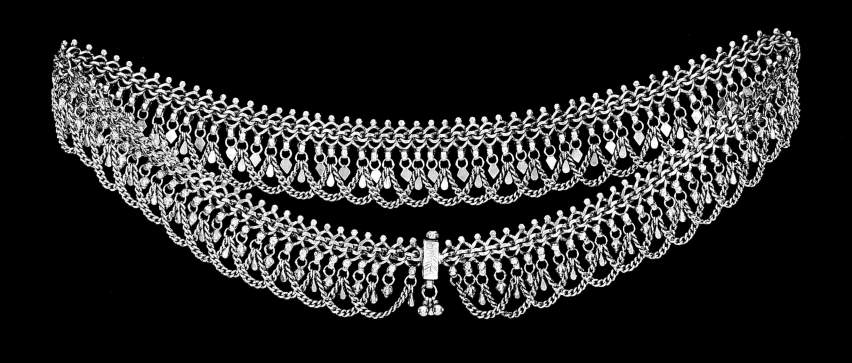

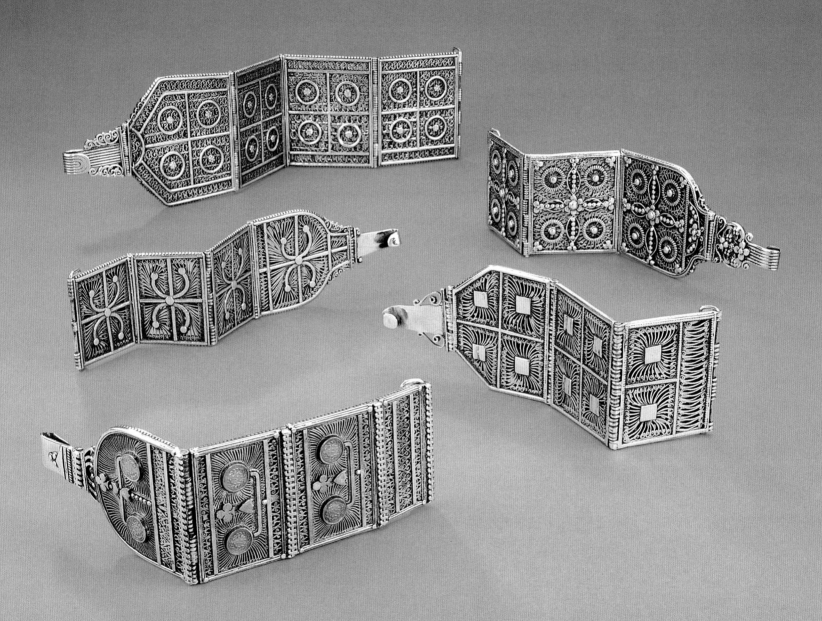

153

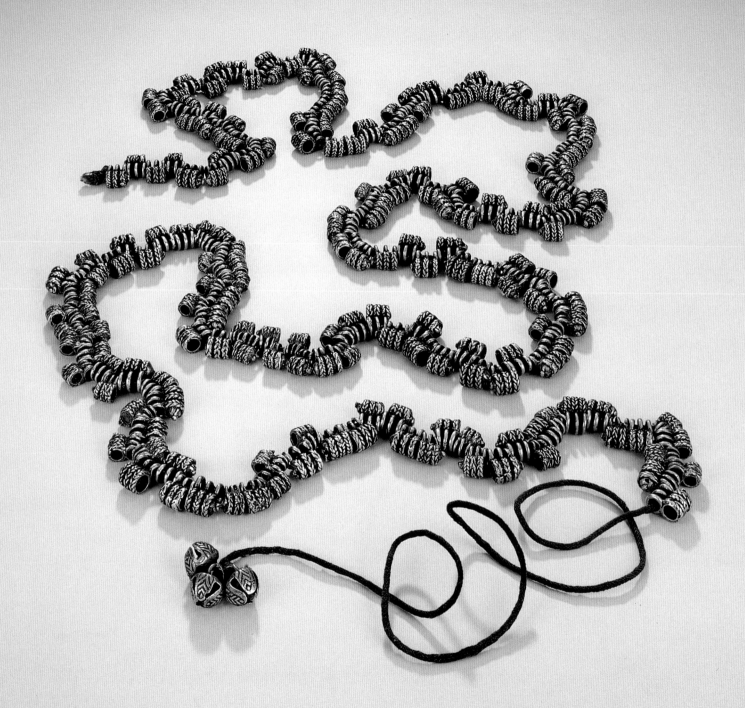

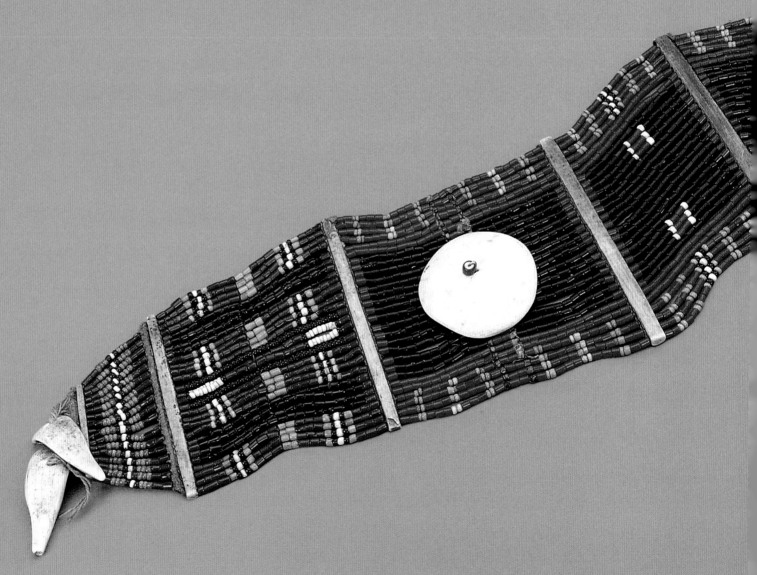

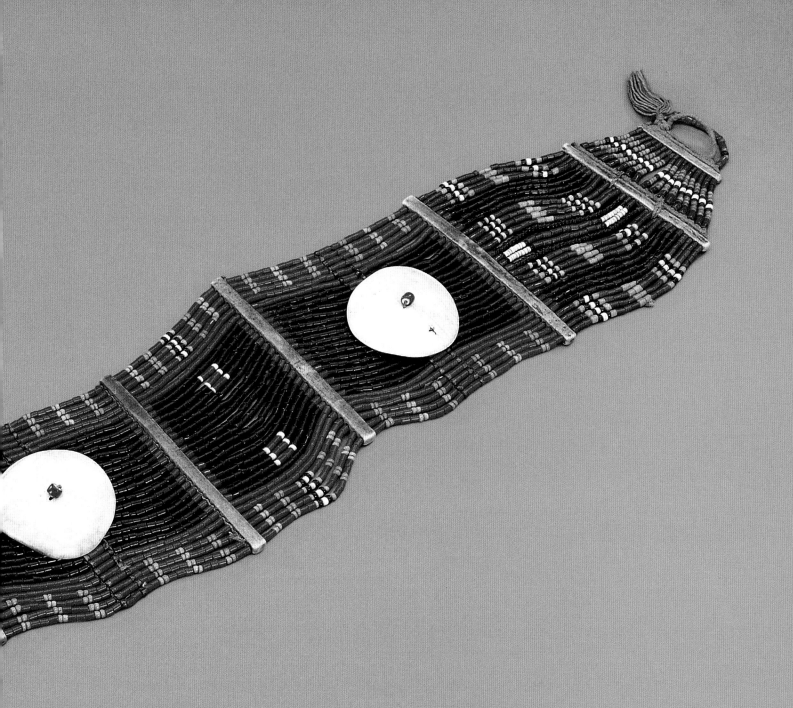

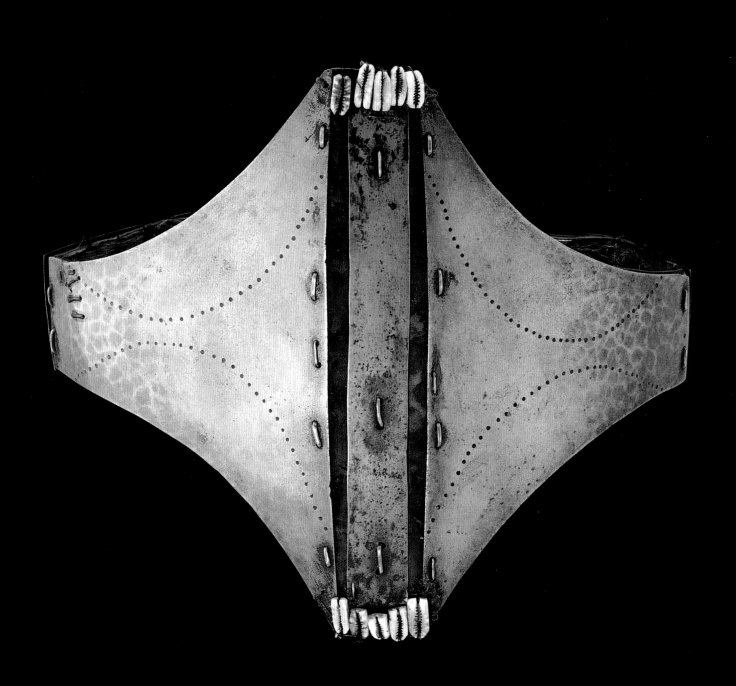

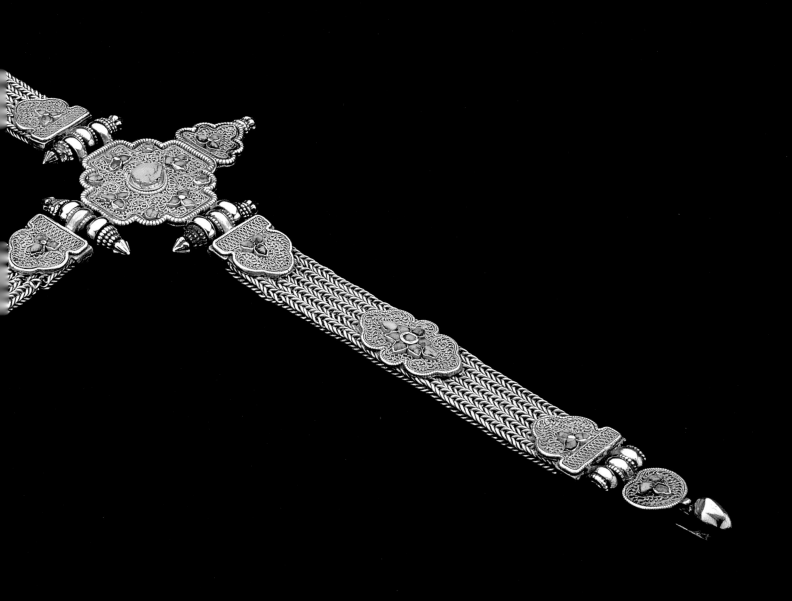

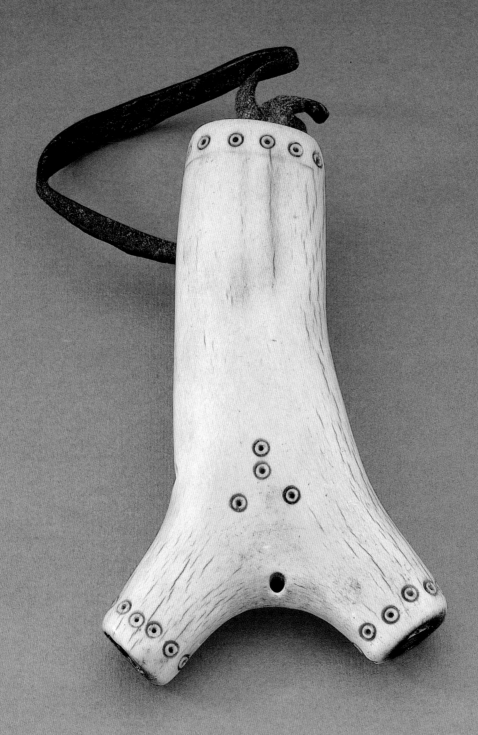

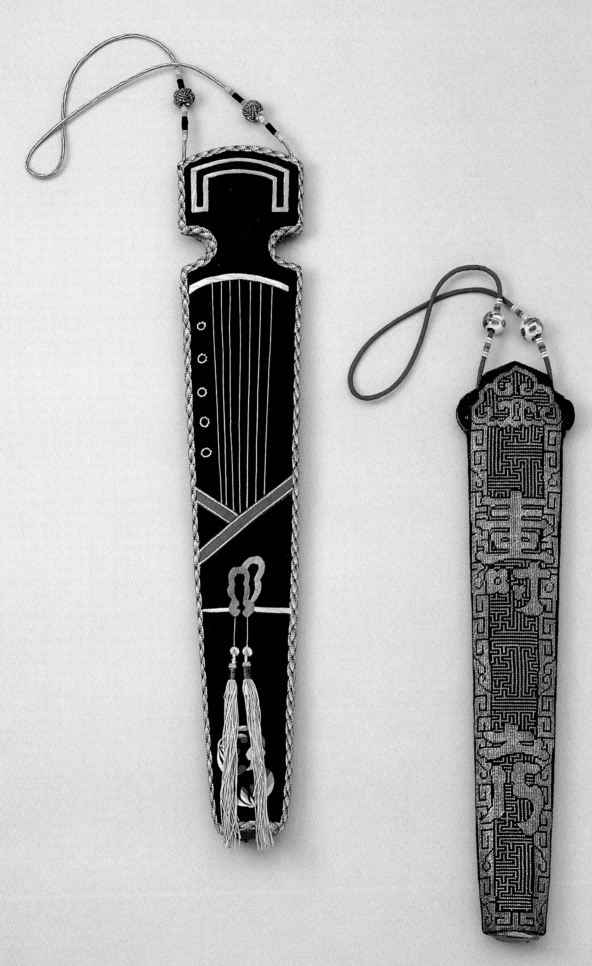

179

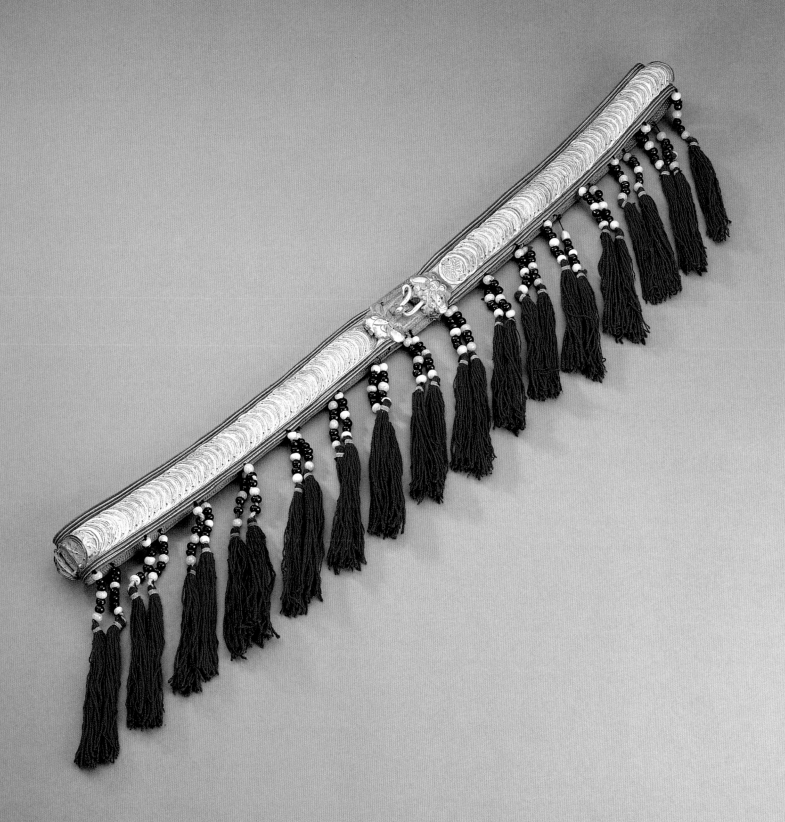

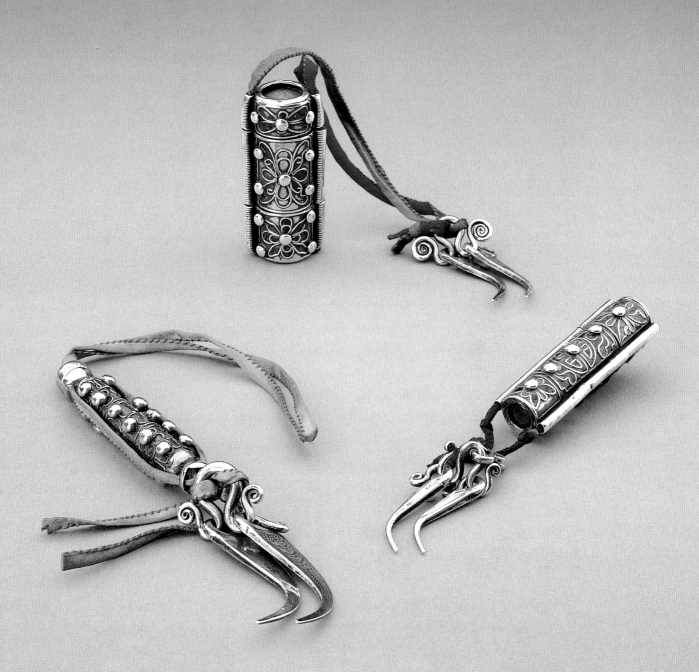

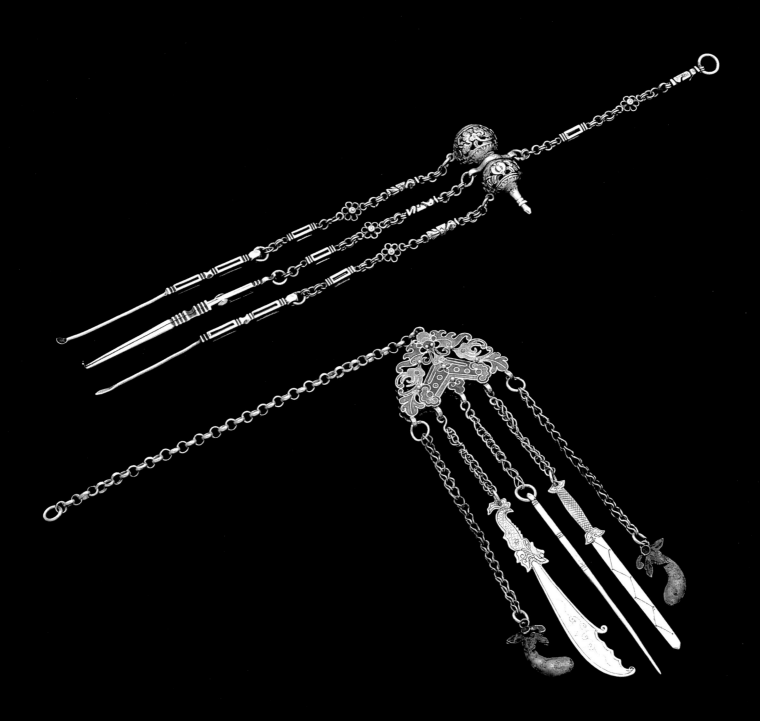

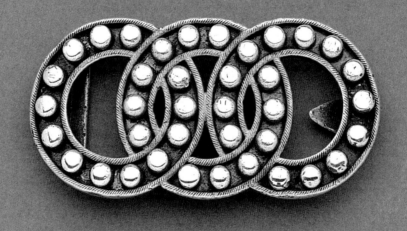

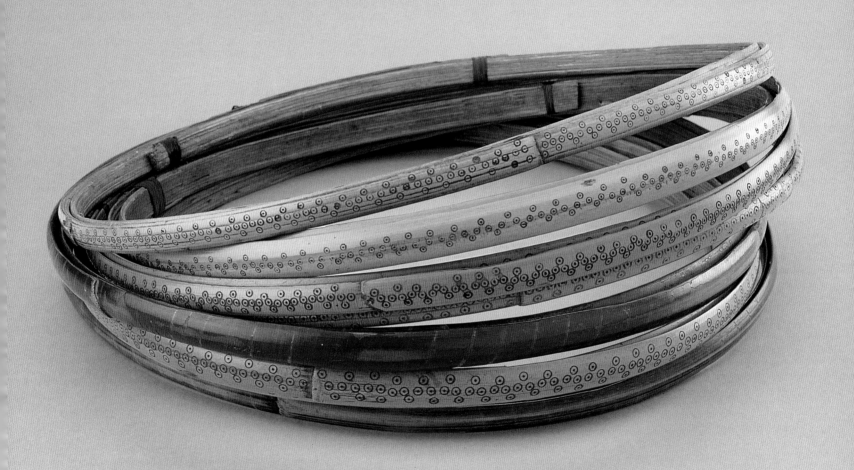

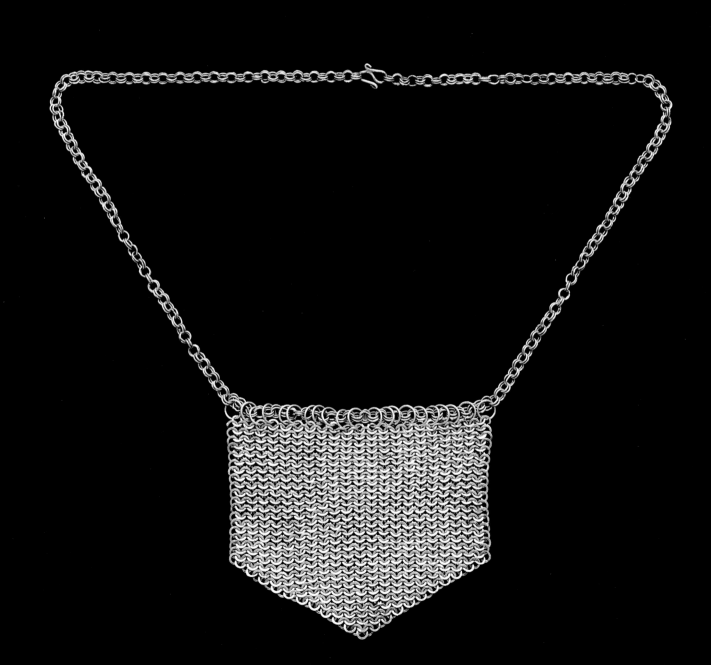

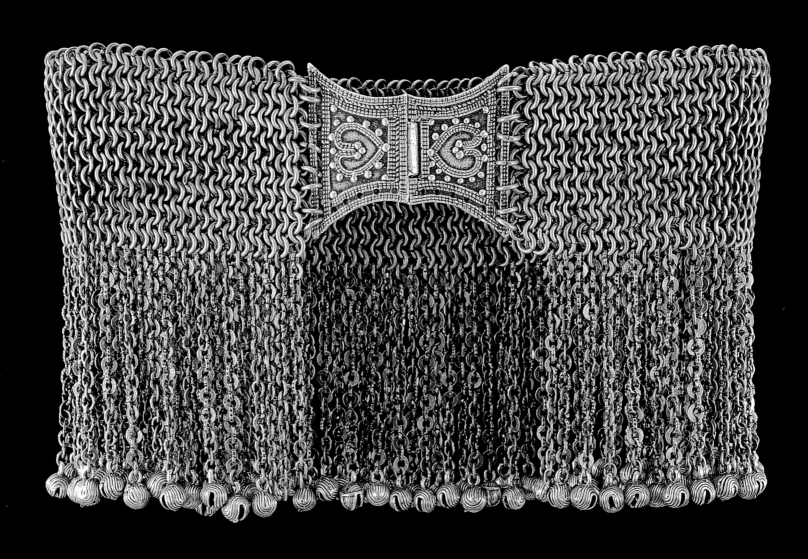

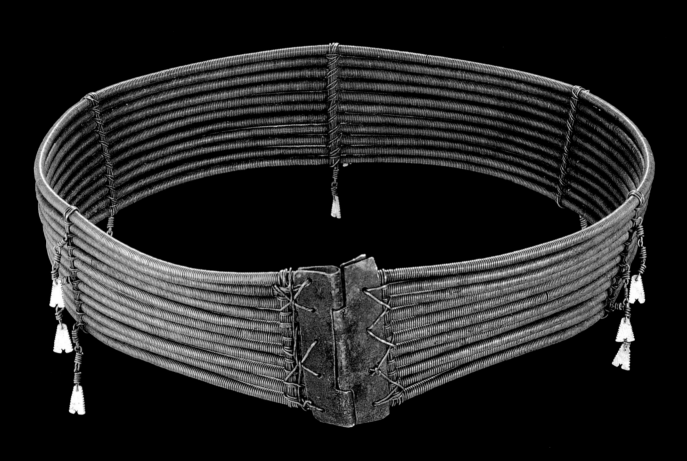

215

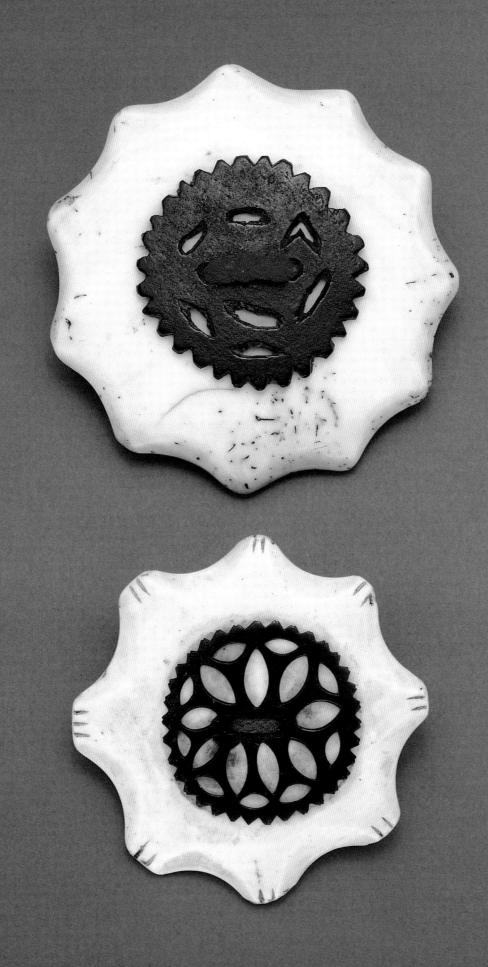

223

228

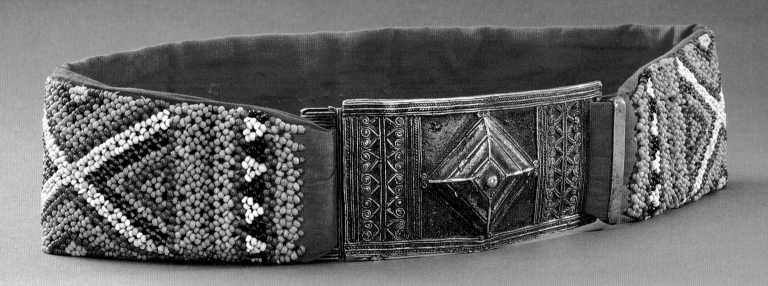

237

239

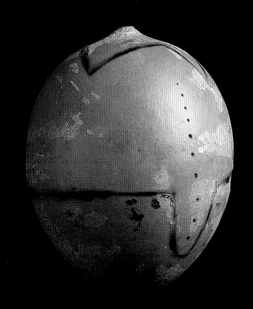

Oceania

Oceania

Gauguin was 43 when he landed in Tahiti in 1891. He came from Brittany, which at the time was still a bigoted, superstitious land of legends. What was he looking for in Tahiti, and later in the Marquesas, if not the promise of an idyllic paradise that the navigator Louis-Antoine de Bougainville had described as a *Nouvelle Cythère* in his eighteenth-century *Voyage autour du monde*[1].

This vast expanse of ocean dotted with thousands of islands, the biggest of which is New Guinea, was gradually colonized by people from Southeast Asia who spoke Austronesian languages. Less than a century ago, most of the ethnic groups still wore *cache-sexe* and all the attributes—body painting, tattoos and jewellery—required for the proper functioning of the institutions in their respective societies. The bamboo penis sheath worn by the Papuans reached a length that equalled the symbolic importance of their virility, which was associated with political power. Other, more modest, *cache-sexe* were made of interlaced palm fibres. Aprons made of a mesh of glass beads in bright colours and geometrical patterns were typical of men's attire in Geelvinck Bay, northwest New Guinea (pp. 256–7), whereas the women there wore a short shell screen (p. 249).

In Melanesia, a large shell was used to cover the penis (p. 247). Fibre sheaths woven in colourful geometrical patterns are found in the north of Malakula. It is certainly in Oceania that the *cache-sexe* is most likely to disappear: missionaries of all denominations, colonists and, more recently, government agents have all strived to put a stop to their use. It is a matter of decency, and decency has a history; it is a constraint invented by men for men. It is a matter of submitting to codes of behaviour and obeying rules. Among the Papuans in New Guinea, these rules were accompanied by gestures and silence. In the big communal houses where many families lived together, there was virtually no privacy. Among the Achuar in the Amazon, who live in similar houses, turning to face the wall meant a refusal to communicate.[2] According to Bronislaw Malinowski 'the categories of decent and indecent do not exist for Trobriand children. In Melanesia, the genitals as such are not under a taboo.[3] Children are educated little by little, as in New Guinea. Margaret Mead explains that among the Arapesh mountain dwellers, the elders take charge of the children's sex education. The only prohibition is looking at female genitals.[4] In the same way, the forbidden aspect of looking and the violence associated with this is a recurring theme in Western painting. From the bride's fright when the 'sex object' is unveiled in the first-century frescoes in the Villa of Mysteries in Pompeii,[5] to Botticelli's *Birth of Venus*, where the goddess is shielded by her hair, and the modest sheltering hand of Manet's *Olympia*, we run the entire gamut of unveiling. But Gustave Courbet's painting *The Origin of the World* is even now regarded as close to absolute indecency and disconcerts visitors, who often look away in embarrassment. Jacques Lacan, the illustrious French psychiatrist and psychoanalyst who once owned this painting had it covered up by a painting by André Masson. He permitted only a few insiders to look at it. Instead of the violence of a visual encounter, Lacan more subtly unveiled the painting. These examples confirm that the *cache-sexe*, although its use is limited, is nonetheless more complex in its relationship with the body than the belt. It has more complicated, diverse functions. It can even be a commercial item, entering into an extensive trading system. Trade maintains links with neighbouring cultural areas: the circulation of material and spiritual goods augments social status, prestige, power and influence in the world of the living as well as in the world of the dead. In the north of Malo, young women wear belts made of cowry currency, *jom,* as a way of hoarding wealth which will be used in trade.

When her husband dies, a Papuan woman coats her body with mud and wears a large number of necklaces

made of tiny shells throughout the mourning period, which can be very long. When mourning is over, she takes off the heavy necklaces and washes her body then ties a knot in her belt, a gesture which signals her readiness for another husband, whom she will choose among the younger brothers of her dead husband. In this case it is a matter of retying the bonds which will renew her sex life.

In Melanesia, the Solomon Islands and Banks Islands as well as in the Micronesian group of the Caroline Islands, belts are varied and used for specific functions in each ethnic group, but they show formal similarities because the environments that supply the raw materials are much the same. Fibres and shells are commonly used because no metal is available.

Weaving and very fine plaiting have developed over the centuries. The exploration of a language of signs and colourful geometrical patterns—which are woven, as in the apron from Geelvinck Bay—or painted on the surface (p. 251), reveals creativity that is just as rich as that found in all other forms of traditional jewellery.

[1] *La découverte du paradis. Océanie, Curieux, navigateurs et savants*, A. Notter (ed.), Somogy Éditions d'Art, Paris, 1997, p. 23.
[2] Descola, P., *Spears of Twilight: Life and Death in the Amazon Jungle*, Eng. trans. Lloyd, J., The New Press, New York, 1996.
[3] Malinowski, B., *La sexualité et sa répression dans les sociétés primitives*, Petite Bibliothèque Payot, French reprint, 2001, pp. 70–1. Original Eng. ed.: Malinowski, B., *Sexuality and Repression in Savage Societies,* Routledge and Kegan Paul, London, 1927 (reprint 1953).
[4] Mead, M., *Mœurs et sexualité en Océanie*, Terre humaine, Poche, Plon, reprint 1963, Chap. 4 and 5. Eng. ed.: *Sex and temperament in Three Primitive Societies*, 1935.
[5] Veyne, P., Lissarrague E., Frontisi-Ducroux F., *Les Mystères du Gynécée*, Gallimard, 1998, p. 17.

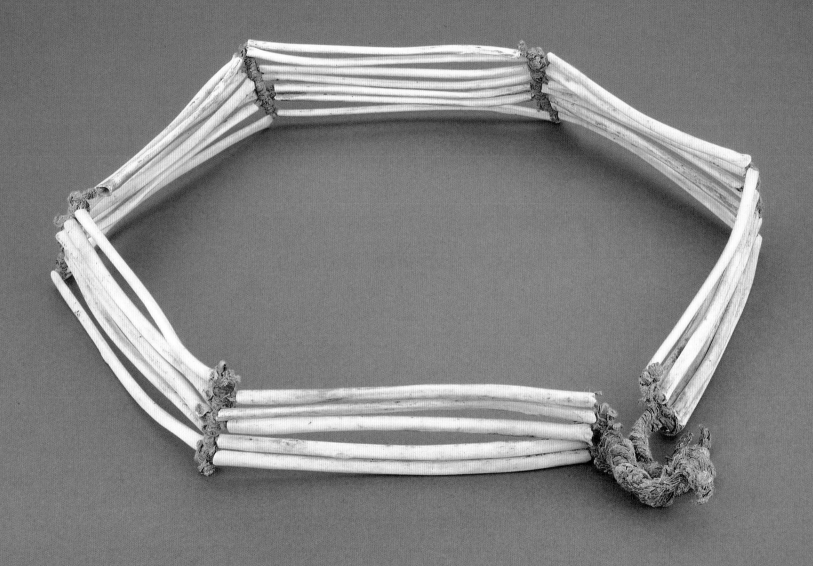

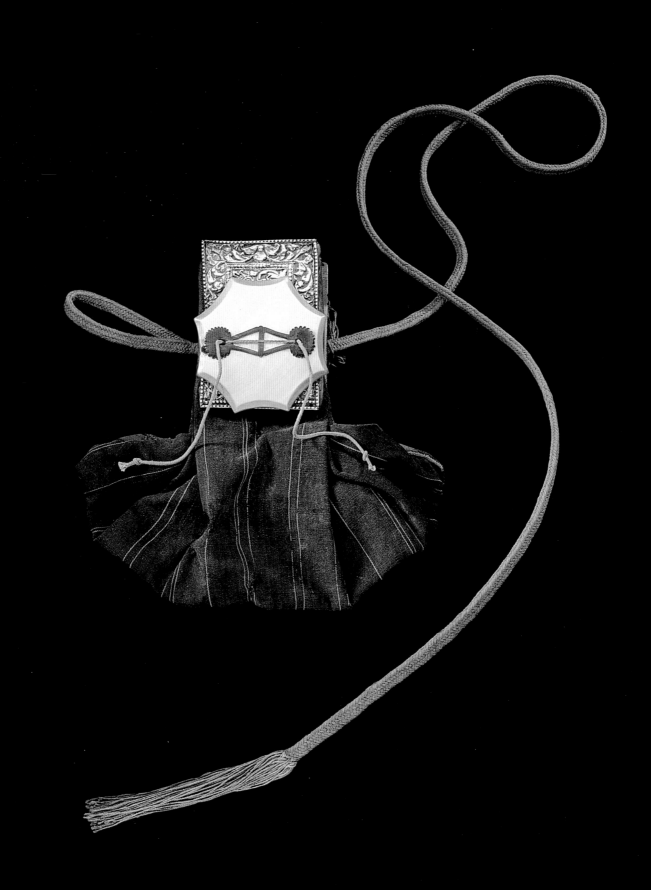

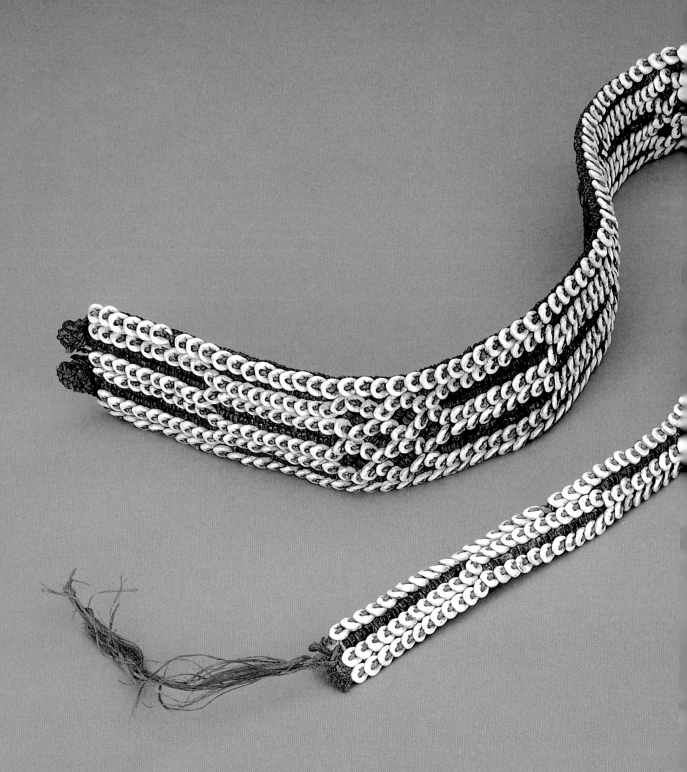

America

North America, Alaska

The Eskimos do not belong to the same stock as the migrants who, over nearly fifteen thousand years, gradually peopled the whole of America. They live in extreme climatic conditions which vary widely with the seasons. Vestiges of their civilisation have been found in ancient tombs and in the remains of their semi-subterranean houses. Objects carved from walrus tusks often show extraordinary artistic skill (Old Bering III, circa 500 AD). Needle cases are utilitarian items still used by the women to sew clothing from seal skins or bladders. The seams of their parkas are ingeniously stitched so they are completely watertight (p. 262). This case is attached through an eyelet to a belt made of a strip of skin. Amulets in the shape of local animals, often bears, could also be tied to the belt.

The Plains Indians

Among the north-eastern tribes, the Iroquois were famed for their tattoos and face painting, which terrified the early colonists. They wore leather clothing embroidered with geometrical patterns by means of porcupine bristles. Apart from the delicate embroidery done by the women, they used large numbers of wampum beads, also known as the 'eyes of the ocean', which they regarded as sacred because they came from the sea.[1] From the sixteenth century on, they made belts to carry messages of war or peace. The arrival of the first Europeans—Dutch, English and French—had a decisive impact on the trade in beads with the introduction of coloured beads (p. 263). The wide range of colours led to the development of a system of communication based on signs that functioned like pictograms, a sort of graphic record of events with comments on conflicts, good intentions and other aspects.

Further south, the Navajo group was famed for the beauty of its silver jewellery which was later decorated with turquoises. The *concha* belt, because of the shell-like elements it is made of, is a sign of wealth and prestige.[2] In the nineteenth century, this belt was worn by the men in the ritual Sun and Moon dance. The silver elements are hooked onto one another (p. 264) or threaded on a leather thong, adorned with finely carved patterns and sometimes decorated with a turquoise cabochon in the centre. Although this type of pattern is of Hispano-Mexican origin, the turquoise, which was used by all the ethnic groups in the south of North America and Meso-America, symbolically recalls the sky and is a sign of health and happiness.

South America, The Amazon

Little is known about the ancient cultures of Brazil except in the Amazon delta, where tombs have revealed the existence of funerary pottery covered with indecipherable signs, and *tanga cache-sexe* imitating the form of a shell (p. 267), whereas in New Guinea a real shell is used as a *cache-sexe*.

Within the huge forest there are surviving groups of Indians, hunter-gatherers whose territories are gradually being whittled away. Where there is no archaeological evidence, ethnography has taken over. Much research has been carried out on one group called the Kaiapo, particularly on their use of finery.[3] Parrot and macaw feathers are used in all their rites and ceremonies, according to strict codes. In this ritual, symbolic theatre, 'bird men' celebrate the spirits of the forest and the land. Ceremonial belts (pp. 276–7) play very specific roles. They may also be made of glass beads, combined with body painting when they are worn by boys. The women prefer slings, wide belts for carrying things, made of glass beads and shells. They exhibit them at the maize festival, the most solemn feast of all, which is the last in a series of rituals. Others, decorated with little bells or shells as among the Jivaro, jingle like musical instruments in time with the dancers' movements (pp. 272–3). Some of them represent privileges which can be bought and traded. The value of the privileges is carefully calculated, depending on the length and colour of the feathers and even the number of serrations in the remiges. It is hard to imagine a more complicated social and political system in which the status of each person is so deliberately displayed!

And where are their *cache-sexe*? Vanished, obsolete, or outmoded? These days, like all the other groups, the Kaiapo wear shorts…

[1] Dubin L.S., *North American Indian Jewelry and Adornment, From Prehistory to the Present*, Harry N. Abrams., New York, 1999, pp. 174–5.
[2] Ibid., p. 489.

[3] Verswijver, G., Kaiapo, *Amazonie, Plumes et Peintures corporelles*, exhibition catalogue, Musée royal de l'Afrique centrale, Tervuren and Snoeck-Ducaju & Zoon, Ghent, 1992, p. 70 ff.

264

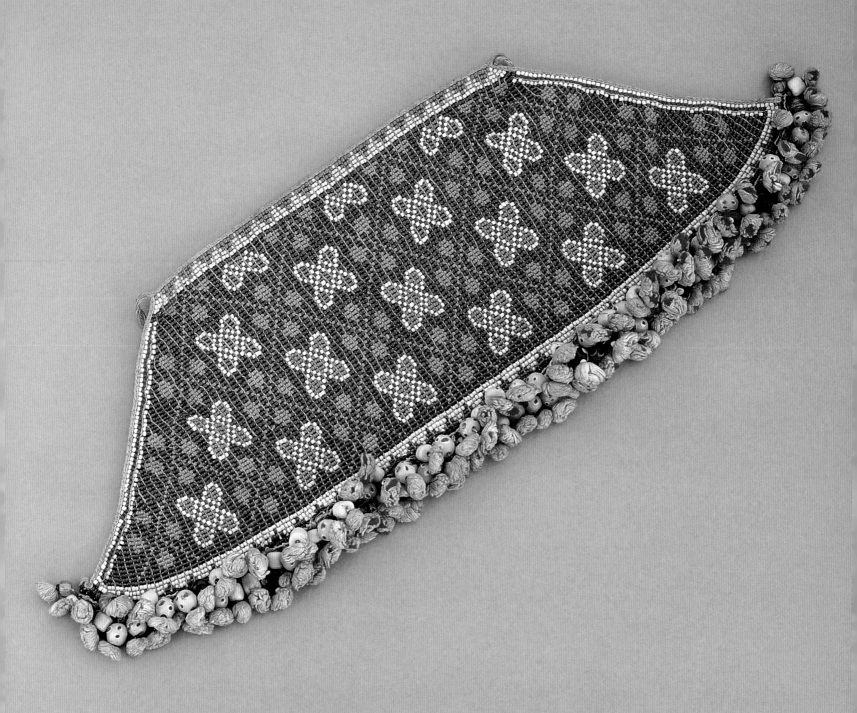

Captions

Africa

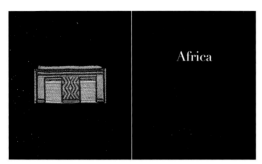

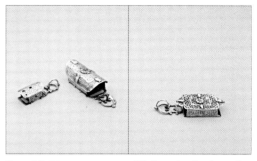

Page 10
*D.R. of the Congo
(Mongo, Mbole)*
Raffia. L. 72.5 cm (belt)
and 8 cm (detail)
The central motif of a
girl's belt, woven from
natural raffia and dyed
brown. Worn on the hips.

Page 15
Morocco, Fez
Silk and gold threads.
L. 350 cm
A ceremonial *hezam*
brocade belt worn by the
bride at her wedding.
Made by Fassi craftsmen
specialized in this kind
of work, the belts are
produced in various
colours and patterns to
suit the woman's
costume.

Pages 16–17
Morocco, Essaouira (left)
and *Fez* (right)
Silver. L. 16.5 cm
Fekroun belt buckles used
to fasten the ceremonial
belts worn by the women.
The upper part of the
buckle showing a tortoise
shell (centre), like the
buckle on the right,
is decorated with four
small protective hands,
representing the hands

of Fatima, the daughter of
the Prophet. The buckles
on page 16 were made by
the jewellers of the old
city of Mogador, now
called Essaouira, on the
Atlantic coast.

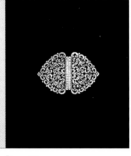

Page 18
Tunisia
Silk. L. 350 cm
A flowing silk *fouta* that
is also found in Morocco.
It is wound around the
waist and tied.

Page 19
Morocco
Silver. L. 9.5 cm
A chased silver belt
buckle with curving
patterns. The goldsmiths
of Mogador were famous
for this fine work.

Page 20
Tunisia
Silver. H. 10.5 cm
Berber women tie the
rings to their belts and
use them to hold their
dresses out of the way
during daily tasks, such
as working in the fields,
which are particularly
arduous in rural areas.

Page 21
Tunisia, Sfax and *Mahdia*
Silver. H. 44 cm
Holga rings which are
more elaborate but used
for the same purpose as
the previous ones. They
are decorated with small
chains ending in hands of
Fatima, which serve as
talismans. They are also
a sign of greater wealth,
because they require more
silver and so are more
costly. The ring on the
right is hollow.

Page 23
Ivory Coast (Baule)
Leather. L. 32 cm
A warrior's belt, made of
partly tanned skin rolled
around several layers of
leather in a complicated
manner.

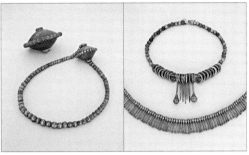
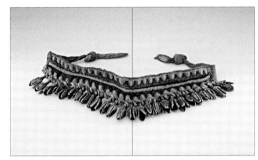

Page 24
Nigeria, Cross River (Vere)
Bronze. H. 40 cm
The Cross River peoples
have been familiar with
iron-casting techniques
for centuries. Women
wear the large double-
coned bead on their
buttocks.

Page 25
Cameroon (Kirdi)
Bronze. L. 75 cm
Above, a belt worn by
girls after their initiation,
from puberty to marriage.
Below, a bronze belt.
Bronze belts, which are
usually reserved for
people of high rank,
require the know-how
of the blacksmith caste.

Pages 26–27
Nigeria
Bronze and cotton.
L. 46 cm
A ceremonial belt
decorated with pieces
of coloured fabric and a
fringe of little bells which
tinkle as the girls dance.

Page 28
Nigeria
Leather. H. 41 cm
Although the material of
this belt is rough, the
technique is refined; it
has dozens of fine leather
plaits brought together in
a clasp with an imposing
button. The leather and
shape suggest that it was
probably a hunter's belt.

Page 29
Nigeria (Mumuye)
Iron. L. 24 cm
A belt pendant, also used
as currency. This one is
large, but the symbolism
of the pattern is obscure.
However, the spiral
evokes the dynamism
of life.

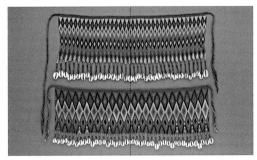
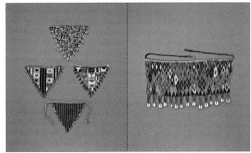
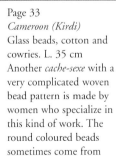
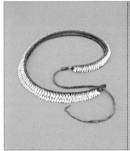

Pages 30–31
Cameroon (Kirdi)
Glass beads, cotton
and cowries. L. 55 cm
Variations on the same
theme, these female
cache-sexe with cowry
fringes for fertility, also
serve as dance skirts.

Page 32
Cameroon (Kirdi)
Glass beads and cotton.
L. 14 cm
The inverted triangle
of these *cache-sexe*,
symbolizing the female
sexual organ, clearly
indicates what it pretends
to hide! It is worn by
little girls.

Page 33
Cameroon (Kirdi)
Glass beads, cotton and
cowries. L. 35 cm
Another *cache-sexe* with a
very complicated woven
bead pattern is made by
women who specialize in
this kind of work. The
round coloured beads
sometimes come from
Venice.

Page 34
Togo?
Fibre and cowries.
L. 78 cm
From ancient times,
cowries—because of their
shape recalling the
vulva—have symbolized
fertility and hence wealth.
Here the craftsman has
delicately arranged them
in two rows to emphasize
the waist; it was probably
made for a woman.

Page 35
Cameroon
Glass beads and cotton.
D. 30 cm
The various dynasties
made abundant use
of local beads, later
importing them from
Europe. Arab merchants
traded in them from the
sixteenth century. These
are old beads.

Page 36
Cameroon (Kirdi)
Fibre, glass beads and buttons. H. 55 cm
An elongated *cache-sexe*, attached to a belt by a fibre tie.

Page 37
Cameroon (Kapsiki)
Leather. L. 21 cm
The Kapsiki, a Kirdi subgroup, live in the Mandara Mountains. Isolated from the rest of the Cameroon by the Fulbe, who are a Muslim group, they maintained their clothing traditions until the mid-twentieth century. The leather is very finely worked.

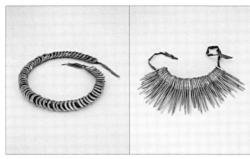 

Page 38
Cameroon, Nigeria (Vere)
Bronze. L. 23 cm
This type of belt is found in northern Cameroon and in north-east Nigeria. The bronze ornaments cast by the lost-wax process are more prestigious than glass beads, even though some of the beads are very valuable.

Page 39
Cameroon, Nigeria (Vere)
Bronze. L. 80 cm
Metal, ivory and glass beads are used to make large pieces of jewellery. Bronze is used instead of gold, which is not found in this area, because it has a similar lustre.

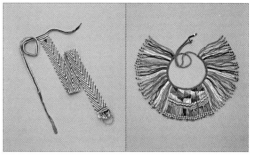

Page 40
Cameroon (Kirdi)
Glass beads and coins. H. 74 cm
The isolation of the ethnic groups in North Cameroon enabled them to escape Islam and the slavery that the Fulbe, a Peul sub-group from Niger, tried to force upon them: hence the continued use of the *cache-sexe*.

Page 41
Cameroon (Kirdi)
Glass beads. L. 112 cm
A shimmering woman's dance belt. The round blue beads are more plentiful in the north, because they were a valuable trade item and were imported by Arab traders from the sixteenth century onwards.

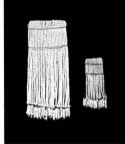 

Page 42
Cameroon (Kirdi)
Glass beads and fibre. H. 28 cm
Cache-sexe varied in type and size depending on the wearer's age, the onset of puberty or changes in social status. Here, the smaller of the two is worn by a girl.

Page 43
Cameroon (Tikar-Bamunka)
Glass beads, wood and cotton. H. 21 cm
A woman's *cache-sexe* worn vertically, attached to a fibre belt by means of a small stick tucked under the belt.

Page 44
Cameroon
Seeds, insect carapaces and fibre. L. 35 cm
These seeds are appreciated for their fragrance. The insect carapaces serve as bells.

Page 45
Cameroon (Matakam)
Iron, cotton and leather. H. 17.5 cm (*cache-sexe*)
This is the most original type of *cache-sexe* used in North Cameroon. It is discreetly erotic, its perfect shape suggesting the mound of Venus under the woman's skirt. It is attached to the leather belt by a curved piece of iron which opens at the sides.

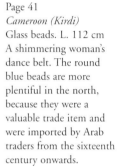  

Page 46
Cameroon
Cowries and leather. D. 22 cm
Although the Kirdi are the best known for a great variety of *cache-sexe*, neighbouring ethnic groups have some fine examples too. Cowries, which are as precious as beads, are used in large numbers. They are attached to skilfully knotted leather thongs and tinkle like bells.

Page 47
Cameroon
Glass beads, cowries, banana seeds and cotton. L. 30 cm
A girl's belt. The Dutch writer, geographer, historian and translator Olfert Dapper (1635–89) recorded the use of sky-blue beads as early as the seventeenth century and compared them to blue river coral.

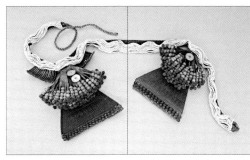

Page 48
Cameroon
Cotton and cowries.
H. 36.5 cm
Cowries sometimes
compete with glass beads.
Their beauty, rarity and
cost put them on a par
with some glass beads,
which gave the owner
extra prestige.

Page 49
Cameroon (Bamileke)
Cowries and cotton.
L. 125 cm
Belt made from a strip of
hand-woven cotton dyed
with indigo. It ends with
two clusters of cowries
which hide the woman's
sexual organs. The
ornament is eye-catching,
no doubt, intentionally
so!

Pages 50–51
Cameroon (Kirdi)
Leather, iron, glass and
iron beads, and coins.
L. 92 cm
It is very unusual to find
such a complete belt.
The *cache-sexe* is usually
made up of a triangle of
leather threaded on a
round leather belt.
Here, the *cache-sexe* and
the buttock apron are
decorated with glass

and wrought-iron beads.
There are also small
comb-shaped iron
ornaments.

Page 52
Chad (Mundang)
Leather, lead and cowries.
H. 33 cm
The Mundang are one
of the pagan ethnic
groups in Chad and
North Cameroon that
were part of the Lere
kingdoms converted
to Islam.

Page 53
Cameroon (Kirdi)
Glass beads and cotton.
L. 67 cm
The waist measurement
suggests that this belt of
beaded strings, serving as
a *cache-sexe* and buttock
apron, was made for a
little girl.

Page 54
Cameroon and *Nigeria*
Iron and fibre. L. 74 cm
Iron was worked in
several stages: the ore was
extracted, cast and
worked by blacksmiths,
who were believed to
have special powers
inherited from the
demiurge of fire. This
man's belt is decorated
with bells which tinkle
when the wearer dances.

Page 55
Cameroon (Matakam)
Iron, leather, cowries
and cotton. L. 41 cm
Like the belt shown
opposite, this rare
cache-sexe is adorned with
wrought iron ornaments.

Page 56
Cameroon
Leather, glass beads
and cowries. L. 72.5 cm
Serving as a *cache-sexe*
and buttock apron,
this belt decorated with
cowries and brightly
coloured beads is for a
mature woman. The size
of the belt and the
materials used are
indicators of the person's
status.

Page 57
Cameroon
Glass beads and cotton.
L. 20 cm
This pubic cover, dyed
in a geometrical pattern,
illustrates the infinite
variety of *cache-sexe* worn
by women in the
Cameroon.

Page 58
Ethiopia, Wollo
Glass beads, silver
and cotton. L. 70 cm
As early as the fifteenth
century, glass beads from
Europe were traded for
local products. Their
colours function as
a system of signs.

Page 59
Kenya (Masai-Chamus)
Glass beads, fibre, brass
and calf tails. L. 161 cm
A man's belt. Each age
group has its specific
jewellery and beads
of particular colours.

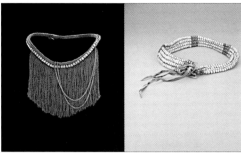

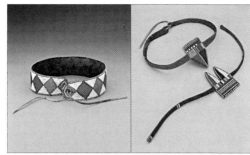
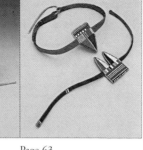

Page 60
Kenya
Leather, fibre and iron.
H. 54 cm
A woman's *cache-sexe*.
Before the introduction
of European glass beads,
iron beads were used.
This rare example has
wrought-iron beads.

Page 61
Kenya (Rendille)
Leather, aluminium
and copper. D. 25 cm
As well as their traditional
materials, the Borana
and the Rendille used
aluminium from old pots
or scrap from aircraft
bodies of western origin
to make jewellery. A fine
example of acculturation!

Page 62
Kenya (Masai)
Leather and glass beads.
D. 25 cm
Beads are a multicoloured
medium for sending
coded messages about the
god of creation, linked to
black, while the earth is
associated with red.
Mixed colours were used
for secondary messages.

Page 63
Kenya (Masai)
Leather and Glass beads.
L. 70 cm
People of the *moran* grade
were allowed to wear a
pale blue belt made of
tiny glass beads. It held
their robes and a dagger.
A beaded motif was worn
in the small of the back.

Pages 64–65
*D.R. of the Congo
(Mangbetu)*
Fibre and banana leaf.
L. 30 cm
The *negbe* buttock apron
was made of pressed,
dried banana leaves, and
attached to a belt. It was
sometimes embroidered
with fibre threads in
natural colours or dyed
black, or decorated with
abstract patterns in the

same leaf, also dyed
black, as illustrated
opposite. Women were
anxious to own a fine
buttock apron. The most
experienced women
helped others make them.

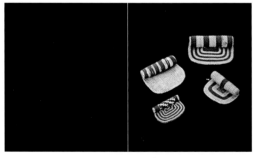

Page 67
*D.R. of the Congo
(Mangbetu)*
Fibre and banana leaf.
L. 13.7 cm
A small *cache-sexe*, placed
over a beaten-bark
support, was the pendant
of a large buttock apron,
as required by the
aristocratic notion of
decency.

Page 68
*D.R. of the Congo
(Mbole?)*
Fibre. L. 110 cm
This is a woman's belt
that is smaller than a
man's belt, but it carried
privileges and was
associated with initiation.

Page 69
D.R. of the Congo
Raffia. L. 113 cm
Very sophisticated
weaving, but
unfortunately the
symbolism of the patterns
eludes us.

Page 70
D.R. of the Congo (Luba)
Raffia. L. 49 cm
There is a surprising
variety in *cache-sexe* made
from natural fibres.
This garment, made for
a woman, is also
a buttock cloth.

Page 71
D.R. of the Congo
Raffia. L. 82 cm
Apart from the fact that
it hid the genitals, little
is known of the
circumstances in which
this traditional fringed
raffia belt was worn.
It may have been a
circumcision garment.

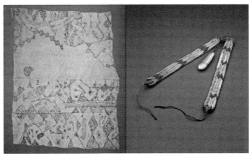

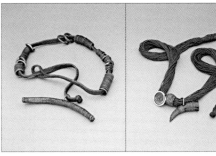

Page 72
D.R. of the Congo (Wagenia)
Fibre, glass beads and brass. L. 75 cm
This belt, which was worn by both sexes, may have come from South Africa. The links, made of a tiny strip of brass, are arranged in a herringbone pattern which produces a very distinctive effect.

Page 73
D.R. of the Congo (Bwaka?)
Leather and copper. H. 40 cm
Leather was not commonly used for belts in central Africa. It was kept for hunters.

Page 74
D.R. of the Congo, Ituri (Bambuti)
Bark and pigment. L. 59 cm
Made in a single piece from beaten bark and painted, such cloth is worn by the Bambuti Pygmies, sometimes folded in half, attached to a fibre belt, sometimes passed between the legs and tied at the waist.

Page 75
D.R. of the Congo (Lega)
Fibre, glass beads and ivory. L. 73 cm
The belt of a woman who had achieved the highest grade in the *bwami* secret society, *kanyamwa ke idul*, comparable to that of the men, which explains why it is adorned with an ivory phallus.

Page 76
D.R. of the Congo (Kuba)
Fibre, copper, brass and wood. L. 124 cm
A belt worn by men, with a very special weave.

Page 77
D.R. of the Congo (Kuba)
Fibre, horn, shell and brass. L. 140 cm
The piece of cone shell and horn suggest that this is a hunter's belt. It is made in a similar way to the belt on the next page.

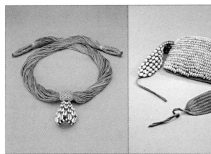

Page 78
D.R. of the Congo (Kuba)
Fibre and cowries. L. 71 cm
A *yet* or ceremonial belt, which is fastened at the back. The king wore one or several such belts to hold his skirts in place.

Page 79
D.R. of the Congo (Kuba)
Fibre and cowries. L. 82 cm
The belt of a high-ranking woman decorated with several rows of cowries. It secured her *ntchak* (woman's skirt) which could reach up to eight metres in length. It was woven and decorated with appliqué work or embroidered with abstract patterns.

Pages 80–81
D.R. of the Congo (Kuba)
Fibre, glass beads, cowries and metal. L. 120 cm
This is a large set of beaded belts for royal use. The cowry rosettes seem to be purely ornamental. The ram's head is one of the many pendants and amulets that slide along royal belts.

Page 82
D.R. of the Congo (Kuba)
Fibre, glass beads and cowries. L. 222 cm
The belt of a woman belonging to the royal family. It is entirely covered with cowries as a symbol of fertility.

Page 83
D.R. of the Congo (Kuba)
Fibre, glass beads and cowries. H. 19 cm (beaded triangle)
The Kuba king enjoyed status that conferred sacred powers on him. He had to be protected physically and mentally. He may have as many as twenty or thirty of these ornaments on his belts.

Page 84
D.R. of the Congo (Kuba)
Shell and leather.
H. 16 cm
This large *iyol* shell
(cowrie) is a symbol
of eternity and in this
capacity is used as an
amulet on a *yet* belt worn
by members of the royal
family.

Page 85
D.R. of the Congo (Luba)
Glass beads and copper.
L. 45 cm
A dignitary's belt.
A tortoise with a
wrought-iron nail in the
shape of a head. Nails like
this one are found in the
hair of statues made in
the Lukuga workships.

Page 86
South Africa (Bushmen)
Fibre, cotton and bone.
L. 26 cm
Living a nomadic life in
a hostile environment,
the women have few
materials for making
ornaments. Sometimes
they use animal bones
as beads.

Page 87
Namibia (Himba)
Leather and iron.
L. 67 cm
Himba women smear
their bodies with a greasy
ointment which rubs off
on their belts and other
pieces of finery. Unlike
Masai women, they still
use the old iron beads.

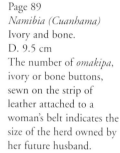

Page 88
Namibia (Himba)
Iron, seeds and plastic.
H. 77 cm
Nomadic herdsmen
sometimes use new
materials out of sheer
curiosity. First glass beads
and buttons, then after
the Second World War,
plastic from irrigation
pipes. It's all grist to the
mill!

Page 89
Namibia (Cuanhama)
Ivory and bone.
D. 9.5 cm
The number of *omakipa*,
ivory or bone buttons,
sewn on the strip of
leather attached to a
woman's belt indicates the
size of the herd owned by
her future husband.

Page 90
South Africa (San)
Ostrich eggshell and
cotton. L. 41 cm
An unusual old example
of a *cache-sexe* made
entirely from polished
ostrich eggshell beads.
Probably worn by
women.

Page 91
South Africa (Bushmen)
Leather and ostrich
eggshell. H. 24 cm
A *cache-sexe* made of
leather, decorated with
small ostrich eggshell
beads. They were
perfectly calibrated and
polished then threaded
on an animal tendon. It
has a matching necklace
which makes a set.

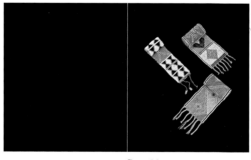

Page 93
Mozambique and *Malawi*
(Yao and *related groups)*
Glass beads, leather and
fibre (left), glass beads
and cotton (right).
L. 80 cm
Like the Zulu, the Yao
use the colours and
patterns of their
beadwork as a form of
communication.

Page 94
South Africa (Sotho)
Fibre and glass beads.
L. 82 cm
A belt that young women
wore low on the hips
so the fringe covered the
pubes. The size of the
beads, which are listed
in catalogues for local
merchants, show that
they come from Europe.

Page 95
South Africa (Zulu)
Banana leaf. D. 5.5 cm
Like some Pacific
Islanders, the Zulu use
this ornament to decorate
rather than hide their
penis.

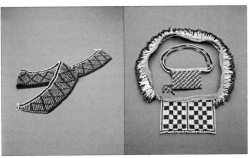
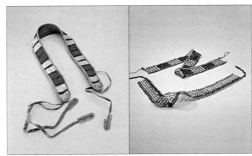

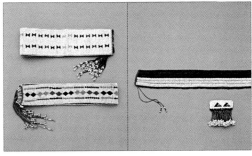

Page 96
South Africa (Sotho)
Fibre and glass beads.
L. 80 cm
The variation in the size of the beads used in this belt shows that it is Sotho. However, a woman marrying a Zulu or Xhosa man sometimes adopted the style of those groups.

Page 97
South Africa (Zulu)
Fibre and glass beads.
L. 88 cm
Cache-sexe worn by nubile girls. Before glass beads were introduced, a variety of less colourful materials were used. The Zulu kingdom flourished with the bead trade.

Page 98
South Africa (Zulu)
Leather, fibre and glass beads. L. 77.5 cm
The patterns used in beadwork spread to other areas thanks to the women who design and make the belts, and then take the patterns with them when they marry. The whole composition conveys a message.

Page 99
South Africa (Zulu)
Fibre and glass beads.
L. 73 cm
An openwork pattern showing the skill and creativity of some of the women who hand down their knowledge to their daughters. These belts are worn on the hips over a leather skirt, which was a married woman's prerogative.

Page 100
South Africa (Zulu)
Leather, fibre and glass beads. L. 64 cm
A girl's belt with pale patterns on a white background. The colours suggest a Xhosa provenance. The diamond pattern is similar to Sotho work in the south.

Page 101
South Africa (Zulu, above and *Ndebele,* below*)*
Fibre and glass beads (above); cotton and glass beads (below). L. 89 cm
The belt is Zulu and the tiny *ligabi (cache-sexe)* belongs to a Ndebele girl.

Page 102
South Africa, Transvaal (Ndebele)
Leather, glass beads and brass. H. 57 cm
A *lipotho* or two flaps apron which symbolizes the couple. The small ties between the two pieces indicate a happy marriage and the hope of many children.

Page 103
South Africa, Transvaal (Ndebele)
Leather, glass beads and brass. H. 76 cm
A five flaps ceremonial *ijogolo* apron, worn by married women. It is given by a woman to her daughter-in-law when she considers her worthy of her son.

Asia

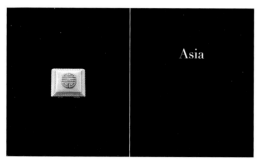

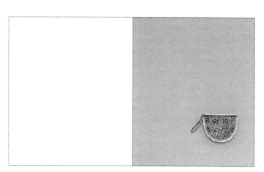

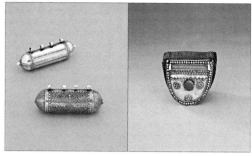

Page 104
China
Ivory. L. 4.7 cm
Belt buckle with an ideogram in the middle, symbolizing longevity.

Page 111
Yemen
Silver. L. 8.5 cm
A *marfazah* used by the men to hold small items. It was attached to a belt and indicated the wearer's social status.

Page 112
Yemen
Silver. L. 15 cm
These plain or richly decorated cylindrical boxes were attached to men's belts and contained thalers.

Page 113
Yemen
Leather, silver and cornelian. L. 12 cm
A purse attached to a man's belt. Cornelian, which was commonly used in Yemenite jewellery, brings luck.

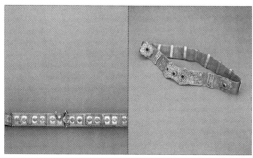

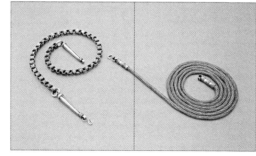

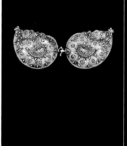

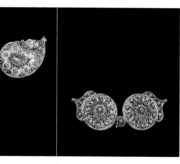

Page 114
Yemen, Hadhramaut
Silver and cloth. L. 84 cm
A woman's belt with various units threaded on a strip of cloth or leather. This type of belt is also found in Oman.

Page 115
Yemen
Silver and glass beads. L. 85 cm
A superb woman's belt, made by excellent Jewish craftsmen. The buckle is decorated with glass cabochons while the other elements are attached to a silver mesh which is used instead of a woven base.

Pages 116–117
Yemen, Socotra Island
Silver. L. 113.5 cm and 300 cm
These belts show an Indian influence, which is hardly surprising considering the volume of trade between the two countries. Socotra Island is one of the largest islands in the Indian Ocean and has held a key position there since the sixteenth century.

Page 118
Turkey, Safranbolu
Silver and enamel. L. 22.5 cm
A belt buckle with filigree motifs and enamel work, used to fasten a silk brocade belt. It is a variant of the following belt.

Page 119
Turkey, Safranbolu
Silver gilt and coral. L. 21 cm
A style typical of the jewellers working in the city in the eighteenth and nineteenth centuries. Safranbolu was one of the two centres which spread their know-how throughout the Balkans in the Ottoman period.

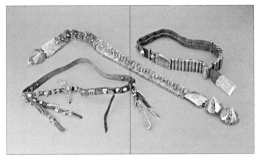

Pages 120–121
Turkey, Van (left)
Silver, niello and leather.
L. 80 and 87 cm
The use of niello
and elements mounted
on a leather base is
reminiscent of belts
from the neighbouring
country of Armenia.
The ceremonial
belt buckle (right)
shows how important
filigree work was

in eighteenth-century
Ottoman jewellery.

Page 122
*Azerbaijan,
(Kabardinians)*
Silver, niello and glass
beads. L. 20.5 cm
Women wore a long
jacket over their bodices,
held in at the waist by the
buckle of the rigid belt
that served as a small
corset.

Page 123
Caucasus
Silver, niello, cornelian
and glass beads.
L. 28.5 cm
Woman's belt buckle with
niello arabesques. Its
remarkable refinement is
an indication of the
owner's high social status.

Pages 124–125
Caucasus
Silver, silver gilt
and leather. L. 84 cm
Men's belts are usually
narrower. The men wear
daggers on their belts as a
distinctive male attribute.

Page 126
Armenia
Silver, silver gilt and
niello. L. 80 cm
A magnificent belt
demonstrating the
craftsmanship of
Armenian jewellers, who
were as famed as the
Georgians. It makes their
ceremonial dress even
more dazzling.

Page 127
Armenia
Silver, silver gilt
and niello. L. 90 cm
Although stylistically
different from Caucasian
belts, Armenian belts—
which are made up of
elements threaded on a
leather thong—have the
same function of
indicating social status.

Page 128
Azerbaijan (Tartars)
Silver and niello.
L. 71 cm
Woman's belt with
jigsawn motifs, most
of which are nielloed.
The buckle is decorated
with a tiny dagger, like
those used by the men.

Page 129
Uzbekistan, Bukhara
Silver, silver gilt and
leather. L. 105 cm
Bukhara jewellers have
been known for centuries
for the quality of their
gold work. This Khan
belt was worn over the
sumptuous silk brocade
or *ikat tchapan*.

Page 130
Uzbekistan (Nogaians)
Silver, silver gilt,
turquoise and glass beads.
L. 83 cm
Each filigree element is
welded to a hinged plate
which makes the belt
more flexible. The
turquoise colour wards
off the evil eye.

Page 131
Uzbekistan, Bukhara
Silver, silver gilt and glass
beads (above), turquoise
(below). L. 25 cm
Blue was a common
colour in Tamerlane's
ancient capital: it was
used on the domes of
mosques and on mosaic
walls, as well as in
jewellery.

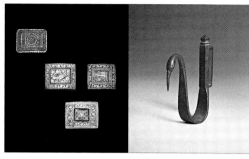

Page 132
Dagestan and Azerbaijan
Silver, leather and glass beads. L. 80 cm
A broad leather belt covered with coins which display its owner's wealth. The buckle is embellished with glass beads in Islamic colours.

Page 133
Uzbekistan
Silver, silver gilt, turquoise and glass beads. L. 7.5 cm
The use of metals combined with a mosaic of turquoises and glass beads in this belt buckle is characteristic of Bukhara; it is a legacy of the splendid jewellery of the Timurid dynasty.

Page 134
Afghanistan (left) and *Kyrgyzstan*
Iron and gold. L. 10 cm
Kirgiz buckles are made of iron damascened with gold, which enhances the belt worn by these fearless horsemen. The openwork pattern on the Afghan buckle is in Muslim-Arab style.

Page 135
Northern India
Iron. H. 10.5 cm
Although iron is not an easy metal to work, the craftsman has made an elegant bird shape. It was attached to a man's belt and used to hold various articles that needed to be easily accessible.

Page 136
India, Maharashtra
Silver. L. 89 cm
This belt with its lotus flower counterweight was designed to accentuate the beauty of the female body.

Page 137
India, Madhya Pradesh
Silver. L. 83 cm
A woman's dowry, *stridhana*, always included a large amount of jewellery and other ornamental items, including belts.

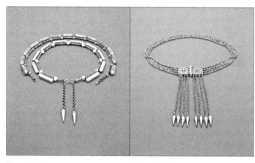

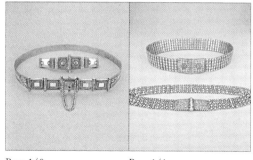

Page 138
India, Kerala
Silver. L. 69 cm
A series of small talismans, interspersed with beads and bells on little chains, are a reminder of the magico-religious function of this type of jewellery.

Page 139
India, Kerala
Silver. L. 80 cm
There are as many models as ethnic groups. The tinkling of the bells, which are shaped like jasmine buds, was intended to ward off evil spirits.

Page 140
South India
Silver. L. 75 cm
The medallion in the middle of the belt represents Mount Meru, regarded by the Hindu religion as a holy mountain and the axis of the world.

Page 141
India, Madhya Pradesh
Silver. L. 78 cm
The techniques used both on the belt and the buckle are evidence of the excellent craftsmanship of Indian jewellers.

Pages 142–143
India, Maharashtra and Karnataka (upper right)
Silver. L. 93 cm
The curving form of the links realistically imitates a snake, which is a sacred animal in Hinduism, symbolizing fertility. It is also associated with the creation of the world.

Pages 144–145
India, Maharashtra
Silver. L. 72 and 93 cm
These opulent belts give an idea of the quantity of silver required by traditional Indian societies to make the jewels and finery for a woman's dowry.

Page 146
India, Andhra Pradesh and *Tamil Nadu*
Silver. L. 63 cm
A woman's *cache-sexe* in the shape of a *yoni*, decorated with flowers and sometimes a moon, which symbolized fertility and life forces. Similar items are found in Sri Lanka, Malaysia and Indonesia.

Page 147
India, Andhra Pradesh and *Tamil Nadu*
Silver. H. 7 cm
A set of *cache-sexe* for women. Girls wore them from childhood to protect their genitals which were thought to be open to evil spirits.

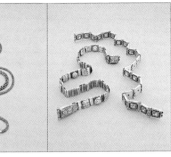

Page 148
India, Maharashtra
Silver. L. 85 cm
The supple, serpentine shape is accentuated by the round model imitating the body of a snake, which symbolizes fertility and is particularly venerated in India.

Page 149
India, Andhra Pradesh
Silver. L. 78 cm
Foliage and animals decorate the various parts of these belts, bringing their wearers good luck.

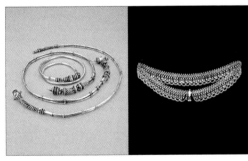

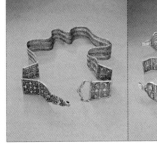

Page 150
India, Maharashtra and *Andhra Pradesh*
Silver. L. 93 cm
This type of screw clasp is one of the most traditional in India. The joints and the fine mesh testify to the jewellers' great inventiveness as well as their technical skill.

Page 151
India, Himachal Pradesh
Silver. L. 83 cm
A woman's belt made up of tiny elements, with little chains and bells that tinkle to ward off evil spirits.

Page 152
India, Kerala
Silver. L. 114 cm
A belt worn by Muslim women; the suppleness of the belt contrasts with the rigidity of the two buckles decorated on the inner and outer sides with different patterns.

Page 153
India, Kerala
Silver and gold. L. 26 cm
A set of buckles like those decorating the belt on the previous page. They illustrate the infinite variety of techniques and decorative motifs invented by Indian jewellers.

Page 154
India, Orissa (Khond)
Bronze and cotton. L. 157 cm
This belt is made of small pieces cast by the lost wax process and illustrates the skill of Indian founders. It is long enough to be wound several times round a woman's waist.

Page 155
India, Arunachal Pradesh
Bronze. L. 57 cm
The *benyop* is worn by a woman until the birth of her first child. It is believed to have been invented by a spirit in love with a mortal woman in order to protect her child.

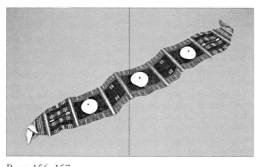

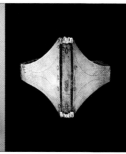

Pages 156–157
*India, Nagaland
(Konyak or Sema)*
Glass beads, shell, bone,
cotton. L. 90 cm
The glass beads that the
Naga use in large
quantities come from
Bohemia and the shells
from the Indian Ocean;
the jewellery is
consequently very
valuable.

Page 158
India, Nagaland (Chang)
Textile, cowries, brass,
wool, bamboo base.
H. 44 cm
Jewellery was the
prerogative of the nobles
and its variety was a
means of identification
like the lace caps worn by
women in Brittany. Each
ethnic group has its own
customs!

Page 159
India, Nagaland (Konyak)
Brass, cowries. L. 28 cm
Used as a corset, this belt
indicated the woman's
social status. The
combination of metal and
cowries was a sign of
prosperity and fertility.

Page 160
India, Nagaland
Bronze, iron, cotton and
glass beads. H. 15.5 cm
A beaded ornament, hung
on a belt, and used
to attach a lime box and
spatula. Lime was used
to prepare betel.

Page 161
India, Andaman Islands
Shell, fibre and pigment.
L. 64 cm
These islands are home
to the last Pygmies in the
South Seas. The Jawara
still wear *cache-sexe* made
of fibre and fine shells,
dyed with the red
pigment they smear on
their bodies.

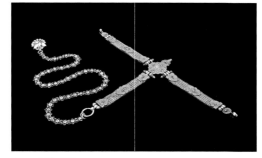

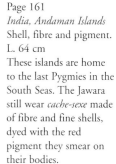

Pages 162–163
India, Ladakh
Brass, silver, leather
and cowries. H. 62 cm
Rows of cowries hung
from a brass disc display
the owner's wealth.
With its continuous knot
pattern, the disc is
a symbol of eternity.

Pages 164–165
Tibet
Silver, gold and turquoise.
L. 41.5 cm; H. 77.5 cm
(chatelaine)
A belt attached on both
sides of the apron
signalling the woman's
married state. The rich
materials indicate that it
was worn on ceremonial
occasions or by a high-
ranking woman. The long
chain topped by a
peacock-shaped hook,
was worn on the upper
part of the bodice, on the
right-hand side.

Page 166
Tibet
Bronze and iron.
L. 50 cm
A belt of exactly the same
design as the previous
one, but worn every day
by most of the women.
A medallion, decorated
with the animals of the
zodiac on the back for
protection, was usually
hung on it.

Page 167
Tibet and *Bhutan* (back)
Silver, copper and iron
gilt, turquoise. D. 8 cm
Boxes for lime (above)
and wax (below); the seal
was used to sign official
documents. The gilded
openwork box in the
centre is characteristic
of Derge.

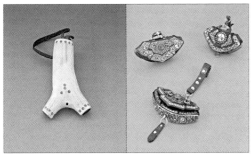

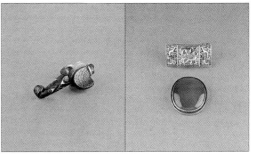

Page 168
Tibet
Bone, leather and
turquoise. H. 15.5 cm
A powder flask in the
shape of an antler, used
by a hunter.

Page 169
Tibet
Leather, silver, silver gilt,
turquoise and coral.
L. 14 cm
Purses for everyday use.
However, the quality of
their silver or silver gilt
ornaments is an
indication of the owner's
wealth.

Page 170
Tibet
Leather, wool, silver
and coral. L. 82 cm
Man's belt made of red
wool, decorated with
cut-out leather ornaments
and chased silver elements
adorned with coral,
which is regarded as
having magical powers.

Page 171
Tibet
Silk, leather and silver.
H. 76 cm
A belt ornament,
consisting of a needle-case
and a purse. This must
have belonged to a
member of the nobility,
judging by the richly
embroidered silk brocade
and the continuous knot
ornament, a symbol
of renewal.

Page 172
*China, Warring States
period* (481-221 BC)
Bronze, gold, silver and
jade. L. 5.5 cm
A belt hook. The
remarkable technique of
inlaying gold and silver in
bronze was developed
during the Warring States
period and reached its
height under the Han
dynasty.

Page 173
China
Gilt bronze, enamel and
cornelian. L. 7 cm
Buckles from the Ch'ing
era (1644–1911).
Cornelian was believed
to have protective powers
and was an indicator of
social rank. The dragon
is a *yang* element,
symbolizing supreme
strength such as imperial
power.

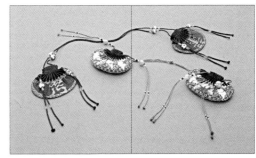

Page 174
China
Jade. H. 6.5 cm
In Chinese Taoist
philosophy, jade is both
yin for its softness and
yang for its hardness.
Inner marbling makes the
stone highly appreciated
as a talisman. Here it is
used as a belt loop.

Page 175
China and *Mongolia*
(above)
Leather, silk, wood
and jade. L. 10.5 cm
These leather pouches
with silk drawstrings were
hung on a belt, often in
pairs. The wooden toggle
and jade pendants repeat
the pattern of the belt.

Pages 176–177
China
Silk, glass beads and
semiprecious stones.
L. 10.5 cm
Embroidered silk purses
worn in pairs on a belt
during the Ch'ing
dynasty. Women kept
perfume and small objects
in them. Their beauty
and the elegance of the
drawstrings are a sign
of wealth.

Page 178
China
Silk, lacquered wood and
shagreen. H. 16.5 cm (case)
In China, glasses are the
sign of a scholar. Shagreen
is the skin of certain sharks
and rays; in France it is
known as *galuchat* because
it was used for the first
time there by a sheath
maker of this name in the
eighteenth century. Earlier
use was recorded in Japan.

Page 179
China
Silk and glass beads.
H. 31.5 cm
Precious, finely
embroidered fan cases,
one in the shape of a
musical instrument.
Such accessories were
the prerogative of
noblewomen.

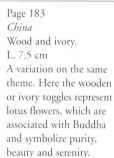

Pages 180–181
China
Ivory. H. 6.5 cm
A set of toggles which, like Japanese netsukes, were used to attach medicine boxes or other small items to a belt. They may be decorated with anthropomorphic, animal, plant or abstract patterns.

Page 182
China
Wood. L. 5.5 cm
A small collection of animals comprising a monkey, a frog or lions of Fo to ward off evil spirits. It must be pleasant to touch, judging by the marks left by centuries of fondling.

Page 183
China
Wood and ivory.
L. 7.5 cm
A variation on the same theme. Here the wooden or ivory toggles represent lotus flowers, which are associated with Buddha and symbolize purity, beauty and serenity.

Page 184
China
Wood. L. 7.5 cm
Bridal shoes for stunted feet, an erotic feature reserved for the ruling class. These miniature shoes were also used as toggles.

Page 185
China
Wood. D. 14.5 cm
Unlike those on pages 186–190, this type of toggle, made of gnarled wood, varied considerably in size and could reach 15 cm in diameter. Similar toggles are also found in Mongolia.

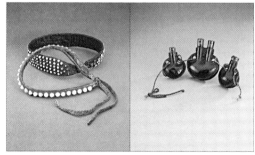

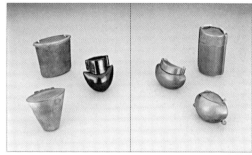

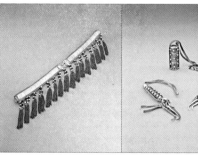

Page 186
China (Yi)
Leather, shell, cornelian and coral. L. 82 cm
One of the oldest ethnic groups in China, the Yi live in Szechwan, on the Tibetan border. The roughness of the natural materials used for the belt contrasts with the elegance of traditional Chinese finery.

Page 187
China (Miao)
Leather, bamboo and fibre. H. 12.7 cm
A set of powder flasks that hunters wore at the waist. These have been made of boiled leather and lacquered.

Pages 188–189
China
Wood, horn and lacquered leather.
H. 8 cm
These stylized tobacco boxes are used by both the men and women of various minority groups such as the Miao.

Page 190
China (Bai)
Silver, cotton and silk.
L. 84 cm
A belt composed of pieces of silver overlapping like fish scales. It is worn by Bai women, one of the minority groups in the autonomous Dali region in Yunnan.

Page 191
China (Miao)
Silver. H. 8.5 cm (case)
Hung on every woman's belt, needle-cases are essential accessories for these nimble-fingered embroiderers.

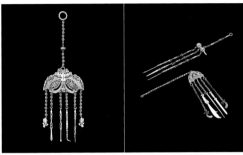
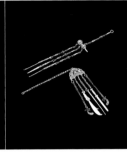
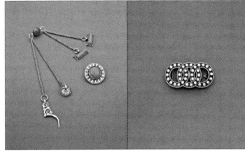

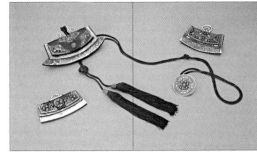

Page 192
China
Silver. H. 38.5 cm
The chatelaine is a Chinese invention, allowing a woman to carry about with her, attached to her belt or her shoulder, a host of small protective or domestic items such as ear cleaners, tweezers and amulets.

Page 193
China
Silver and enamel. H. 32 cm
Two slightly different chatelaines, one with a butterfly (right), and the other with a calabash (left), symbolizing long life.

Page 194
Mongolia
Silver and coral. H. 31.5 cm
This toggle in the form of a lotus flower is accompanied by a small kit containing a pipe cleaner and snuffer, also hung on the belt.

Page 195
Mongolia
Silver and enamel. L. 9 cm
A belt buckle with three interlocking rings symbolizing eternity.

Pages 196–197
Mongolia
Silver, silver gilt, iron, silk, coral, turquoise and lapis lazuli. L. 17 cm
Attesting to the refinement of Mongol jewellery in the eighteenth century, these lighters show high social status and the one on the right is even covered with silk. A flint was struck against the blade to produce sparks that lit the tow. The tow and the flint were kept in the leather pouch.

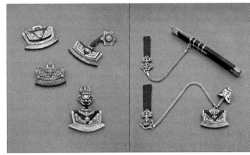

Page 198
Mongolia
Leather, silver, gold and iron. L. 11.5 cm
Another set of lighters, some with a counterweight.

Page 199
Mongolia
Leather, silver and iron. H. 35 cm
Everyday objects, but of a quality that was reserved for the elite. This is a sheath with two knives and a set of ivory chopsticks, along with a matching lighter and its counterweight.

Page 200
Japan
Silver, gold and enamel. L. 5 cm
The *obidome* slides on the *obijime*, a ribbon which keeps the obi in place. The chrysanthemum symbolizes love in the language of flowers. Like the netsuke, it may be the signed work of a great master.

Page 201
Japan
Silk brocade. L. 383 cm
The obi is a sash worn to hold in place several layers of kimonos, garments which do not have any fasteners. The length, material and printed pattern indicate the age and status of the wearer as well as the colour of the season.

Page 202
Japan
Ivory, walnut, wood and silk. D. 4.8 cm
Netsukes varied with social class, ranging from a plain wooden or ivory button to the most refined miniature sculpture. They were used to attach an *inro* (an ornamental box holding seals, medicines, etc.), or a tobacco pouch.

Page 203
Japan
Wood. H. 5.5 cm
Netsukes were carved from cypress, cherry, box or sandal; these precious woods were used for intricately carved objects which scholars collected out of sheer love of beauty.

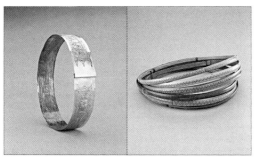
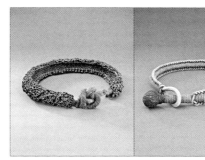

Pages 204–205
Myanmar (Padaung)
Silver and bamboo.
L. 96 cm (left)
and D. 29 cm
The repoussé silver belt
is worn with bamboo
rings decorated with
poker-work. Padaung
women wear a wide
assortment of jewellery,
ranging from the
roughest to the most
refined, which may be
made of gold, silver,
bronze or bamboo.

Page 206
Myanmar
Bronze and cotton.
L. 91 cm
A special woven belt
including tiny bronze
ornaments cast by the lost
wax process, believed to
date from the Pyu period
(first millennium AD).
It could be a ritual belt
assembled by the Shan.

Page 207
Thailand
Cotton. L. 90 cm
The cord belt worn by
Buddhist monks is a
reminder that the founder
of Buddhism, Siddhartha
Gautama, gave up all his
riches—which he
regarded as being just
illusions—to find
the true path to
enlightenment.

Page 208
Thailand (Yao)
Silver and enamel.
H. 40 cm
The Yao prize enamelling
which was invented in
China where this group
originated. A large Yao
community still lives in
China. Signifying long
life, the ideogram is
accompanied by a fish
and a butterfly, both
beneficial animals.

Page 209
Thailand
Silver. L. 54.5 cm
and 8.7 cm (*cache-sexe*)
In rural areas, little girls
wear a *cache-sexe* until the
age of three. The
materials they are made
of—coconut shell, silver
(as illustrated here), or
gold—depend on the
wealth of the family.

Page 210
Thailand
Silver, L. 95 cm
A belt similar in design
to Indian belts.
The chased buckle,
however, is typically Thai.

Page 211
Thailand
Silver. L. 84 cm
A belt with a type of
mesh found from the
Arabian Peninsula to the
Malay Archipelago. It is
worn by various tribes in
the Golden Triangle.

Page 212
*Philippines, Mindanao
(Bagobo or T'Boli)*
Bronze. L. 75 cm
The *sabitan* is worn by
both men and women.
The mesh demonstrates
the skill of the renowned
jewellers of Minanao.
The tinkling bells drive
off evil spirits.

Page 213
Philippines, Luzon (Bontoc)
Mother-of-pearl and glass
beads, coconut shell
and bronze. D. 19 cm
(shell)
The prerogative of nobles
and head-hunters, this
highly valuable ornament
bore decoration that is
similar to the patterns
used for textiles and
tattoos.

Page 214
*Philippines, Luzon
(Ilongot)*
Brass and mother-of-
pearl. L. 69 cm
In the north of Luzon,
belts are part of
aristocratic marriage
agreements, symbolizing
family loyalty and mutual
obligations.

Page 215
*Philippines, Mindanao
(Bagobo)*
Bronze and silver.
L. 61 cm
Gold work, influenced by
metal casting techniques
from Sulawesi and
Borneo, is sacred. The
jewellers work under the
protection of a spirit
known as 'Tolus ka
towangan'.

Page 216
*Philippines, Luzon
(Gaddang)*
Cotton and glass beads.
L. 89 cm
Women have magical
powers which work as
long as the cloth is red
and black and the beads
are red, yellow, black
and white.

Page 217
*Philippines, Luzon
(Gaddang)*
Cotton, glass beads,
copper and silver.
D. 51 cm
When the four prescribed
colours are used together,
they symbolize the
cosmos in which the
upper and lower worlds,
and men and women,
are in equilibrium.

Pages 218–219
*Philippines, Luzon
(Ifugao)*
Shell, cotton, brass and
cane; shell, tortoiseshell
and horn (right).
H. 68 cm, D. 2 cm
A belt to which the *upud*
(opposite) is attached,
along with the *bolo*, a
knife used by hunters and
warriors. The *upud,* made
of a tridacna (giant clam
shell), although worn by

men, represents the
goddess Pumupud, who
watches over difficult
births.

Page 220
*Indonesia, Sumatra, Aceh
(Gayo-Alas)*
Silver. L. 90 cm
A belt made of coins
bearing the head of
Queen Victoria. Coins
have been used in
jewellery since the
Portuguese conquered the
Malay Peninsula in 1511
and the supply became
plentiful through trade.
The fish symbolizes

fertility and, as a result of
this, wealth.

Page 221
Indonesia, Sumatra, Aceh
Silver gilt. L. 83 cm
Sumatran jewellery
combines Hindu
and Buddhist influences,
Islamic techniques and
animist decoration.

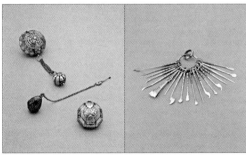

Page 222
*Indonesia, Sumatra
and Sri Lanka (centre)*
Silver and iron. D. 9 cm
Tobacco and lime boxes
used to prepare betel.
The plant decoration is
characteristic of
Indonesian and Malaysian
boxes. The lime box from
Sri Lanka, made of iron
inlaid with silver, has a
matching spatula.

Page 223
Indonesia, Sumatra, Aceh
Silver and *suasa* (a gold
alloy). H. 16 cm
A set of small personal
instruments carried
by men. They are
reminiscent of the
chatelaine worn
principally by women
of Chinese descent.

Page 224
*Indonesia, Sumatra
(Minangkabau)*
Brass, gala and cotton.
L. 27 cm (buckle)
A belt with an austere
looking buckle, worn by a
single man dressing up to
pay court to a woman!
Made in batik, the lotus
flower motif is common
in the area around
Padang.

Page 225
*Indonesia, Sumatra
(Minangkabau)*
Gold and haematite.
L. 25 cm
Sumptuous *pandiëng*
buckles of chased gold
used to fasten silk belts
worn at weddings.
Similar buckles, but set
with precious stones, are
found in Malaysia.

Pages 226–227
*Indonesia, Java
(below left) and Sumatra
(Minangkabau)*
L. 26 cm
Various *pandiëng* buckles
which differ in materials,
size and technique. Those
shown on page 227 are
decorated with magic
squares with from nine to
thirty two compartments.

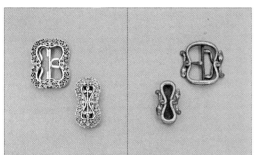

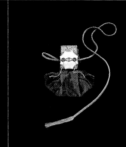

Page 228
Indonesia, Java
Silver, *suasa* (gold alloy), diamonds, iron and gold. H. 8.5 cm
Buckles worn at the *kraton*, or palace, on a black silk belt, embellished with *intan* (diamonds).

Page 229
Indonesia, Java
Iron and gold. H. 7 cm
In Hindu mythology the *naga* (snake) is linked to the creation of the world. It has protective powers.

Page 230
Indonesia, Sumatra, Aceh (centre left) and Sulawesi
Silver and *suasa* (gold alloy). H. 8 cm
In the south of Sulawesi, girls from the Bugis noble families wear *jempang* or *cache-sexe*, which are similar to those from other Indonesian islands, South India and Sri Lanka.

Page 231
Indonesia, Sulawesi (Toraja)
Cotton, silver, mother-of-pearl and tortoiseshell. H. 14 cm
A small purse that men wear at the waist to carry small everyday items.

Pages 232–233
Malaysia, Sarawak, (Iban Dayak)
Brass and cane. H. 18.5 and 24 cm
These corset belts are different from those found in other islands in the Malay Archipelago, where gold and silver are plentiful. The same type of belt is found at Alor in the Moluccas (see p. 239).

Pages 234–235
Indonesia, Nias
Glass beads, brass and bamboo. L. 86 cm
Nobles in Nias share out gold jewellery as the bride price. Glass beads are equally prized and were imported from Venice as early as the fifteenth century.

Page 236
Indonesia, Sulawesi
Bronze, glass beads and cotton. L. 71 cm
As in other islands in the archipelago, beadwork, which is mainly done by the women, is very important in marriage agreements. The buckle is similar to the work of by the Batak bronzesmiths in Sumatra.

Page 237
Indonesia, Sulawesi
Silver gilt. H. 11.5 cm
A belt ornament comprising fruit, a small casket and a crayfish, the symbolism of which elludes us. The very fine filigree work was done by Chinese jewellers for islanders from Alor.

Pages 238–239
Indonesia, Alor
Rattan, bamboo, palm, leather and iron (right). D. 28.5 cm
Bamboo, horn and metal (left). L. 26 cm
The wickerwork belt (right) is similar to those made by the Iban Dayak illustrated on p. 232–3; both types are wide and stiff, imparting a haughty bearing to the wearer.

Oceania

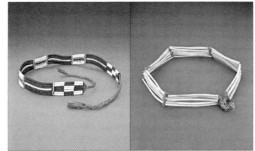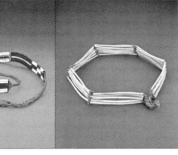

Page 240
*Papua New Guinea,
High Sepik (Amanab)*
Gourd. H. 5 cm
Pyrographed penis sheath,
worn daily. It has
protective and decorative
functions.

Page 244
*Caroline Islands,
Truk* and *Yap*
Shell, coconut shell,
tortoiseshell and fibre.
L. 72 cm
These beads are typical
of men's belts both in
the Carolines and the
Solomon Islands.
They were worn without
any other clothing.

Page 245
Papua New Guinea
Fibre and bone. L. 78 cm
A woman's belt made of
flying-fox bones, a
material commonly used
in New Guinea.

Page 247
Papua New Guinea
Shell. H. 25 cm
Papua New Guinea is a
world apart in the Pacific
Islands. *Cache-sexe*, such
as this penis sheath worn
by an initiate, were
common.

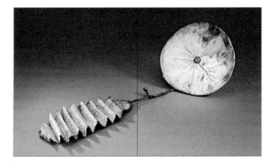

Page 248
Papua New Guinea
Shell, glass beads, fibre
and pigment. H. 53 cm
Glass beads are a greater
sign of wealth than shells,
which are very common
in these hierarchical
societies.

Page 249
Papua New Guinea
Shell and fibre. L. 35 cm
In this region where shells
are the basic material for
jewellery, the setting
is often very elegant, as is
shown in this woman's
cache-sexe.

Page 250
*Papua New Guinea,
Admiralty Islands*
Shell, glass beads, teeth
and fibre. L. 50 cm
A belt which uses tiny
coloured beads and small
teeth as well as minute
shell beads.

Page 251
Papua New Guinea
Fibre, pigment and pigs'
tails. H. 82 cm
A ceremonial apron used
in men's initiation rites.
The ritual colours are
those of the masks.

Pages 252–253
*Papua New Guinea,
New Britain, Gaulim
(Baining)*
Beaten bark and
pigments. D. 24.5 cm
(disc) and L. 75 cm
A *cache-sexe* made of *tapa*,
recently made and still
used by initiated mask
wearers during the fire
dance. The disc covered
the penis and the long
part was put between
the legs and tied at
the back to a belt made
of creepers.

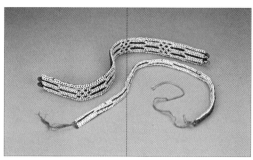 

Pages 254–255
Indonesia, Northern Irian Jaya
Shell, coconut shell
and fibre. L. 67 cm
Belts, some of which have
delicate patterns of *nassa*
and calibrated coconut
shell beads. They are
worn by the men.

Pages 256–257
Indonesia, Irian Jaya, Geelvinck Bay
Glass beads, fibre and
cotton. L. 60 cm
A woman's skirt. Its beads
come from China or
South India and are
highly prized. The bead
mesh is very complicated
to make. This type of
mesh is also found in
Kalimantan and in
Sarawak in Malaysia.

America

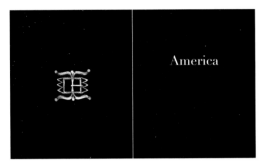

Page 258
United States, Arizona
and *New Mexico (Zuni)*
Silver and turquoise.
L. 8.7 cm
Turquoise has special
status for the Zuni
because it is part of their
mythology. It is believed
to bring protection
and happiness.

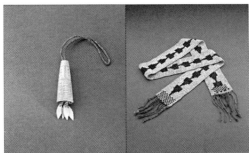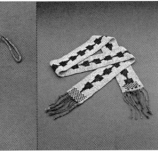

Page 262
United States, Alaska
Walrus tusk and fibre.
H. 9.5cm (case)
The Inuit, of Mongolian
origin, wear belts made
from scraped sealskin
wound tightly around the
parka. The women hang
bone needle-cases from
them.

Page 263
United States,
West of the Great Lakes
(Plains Indians)
Glass beads and cotton.
L. 113 cm
Men's belts were
originally decorated with
shell beads. Glass bead
belts appeared in the
sixteenth century, but the
patterns stayed the same.

Page 264
United States, Arizona
(Navajo)
Silver. L. 94 cm
In the sixteenth century,
Navajo tribes bought
horses, copper and silver
from the Spanish.
The jewellers then used
Mexican pesos. This
concha belt has taken its
shape from the shell.

Page 265
United States, Arizona
(Navajo)
Silver and turquoise.
L. 7.7 cm
Belt clasp with
a turquoise set as
a cabochon. Its mineral
blue colour makes it
desirable and it is believed
to have magical and
spiritual powers.

Page 267
Brazil, Amazonia
Terracotta and pigment.
H. 11 cm
Archaeological excavations
of a site in the Amazon
Delta dating from 400 AD
yielded tomb goods,
including this *tanga*, a
cache-sexe covered with
the same abstract patterns
as the anthropomorphic
jars.

Page 268
French Guyana (Wai Wai)
Glass beads, fibre and
cotton. L. 42 cm
Woman's beaded
cache-sexe woven on
a loom with a backrest.
At first, *cache-sexe* were
made from shell beads.

Page 269
Brazil, Ucayali River,
Panoan
Shell. D. 11 cm
Penis sheath worn during
puberty rites. Its shape
and use recall the much
earlier sheaths used by the
people of the Amazon
Delta in 400 AD.

Page 270
Brazil, Amazonia
Glass beads. L. 96 cm
Used in large quantities,
beads were an impressive
display of wealth. Worn
on the hips and tied
around the pubes, they
generally had a small
ornament on the tie,
which is absent here.

Page 271
Bolivia (Aymara)
Alpaca. L. 174 cm
A woman's *huaka* (belt),
used to hold her *urku*
(skirt) in place. The
patterns and the weaving
technique show some
similarities with work
done in Chile in the first
centuries AD.

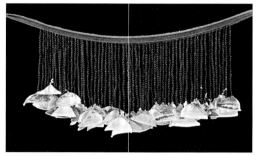

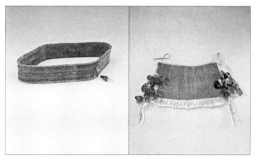

Pages 272–273
Brazil, Amazonia
Shell, seeds and cotton.
Total L. 105 cm
Made, like most finery,
with materials from the
natural environment, this
woman's belt was worn
on the hips during ritual
ceremonies. The shells
rattled in time to the
dancers' movements.

Page 274
Brazil, Amazonia, Xingu
Fibre and feathers.
L. 35 cm
The Xingu comprise a
number of ethnic groups
living north-east of the
Mato Grosso. The
pendant at the front of
the belt, made from two
yellow feathers inserted
in the husk of a piece
of fruit, indicates
a particular status.

Page 275
Brazil, Amazonia
Feathers, seeds and
cotton. L. 50 cm
A *cache-sexe* woven from
tiny seeds, requiring great
skill. It is very
sophisticated and worn
by the women.

Pages 276–277
Brazil, Amazonia (Kaiapo)
Feathers, seeds and cotton.
L. 115 cm
In this highly hierarchical
society, any new status is
indicated by feathers from
macaws and other parrots.
The small feathers used for
this ceremonial belt come
from the breast of
a macaw. They function
as a remarkable coded
language.

Appendix

Europe

Venice

Black Sea

Caspian Sea

Mediterranean Sea

Asia

Morocco
Essaouira

Mahdia
Sfax
Tunisia

Anti-Atlas

Western Sahara

Algeria

Libya

Egypt

Nile

Red Sea

S a h a r a

Mauritania

Mali

Lere

Niger

Chad

Sudan

Nile

Eritrea

Wollo

Djibouti

Senegal

Senegal

Gambia

Niger

Niger

Burkina-Faso

Nigeria

Grasslands

Ethiopia

Somalia

Guinea Bissau

Guinea

Ghana

Benin

Togo

Cross River

Mandara Mounts

Central African Rep.

Sierra Leone

Ivory Coast

Liberia

Cameroon

Uganda

Kenya

Equat. Guinea

Gabon

Congo

Zaire

Ituri

Rwanda

Burundi

Congo

Dem. Rep. of Congo
(ex-Zaire)

Zaire

Tanzania

Zanzibar

Atlantic Ocean

Angola

Zaire

Zambia

Malawi

Mozambique

Madagascar

Zimbabwe

Namibia

Kalahari Desert

Botswana

Transvaal

Swaziland

South Africa

Lesotho

Indian Ocean

N

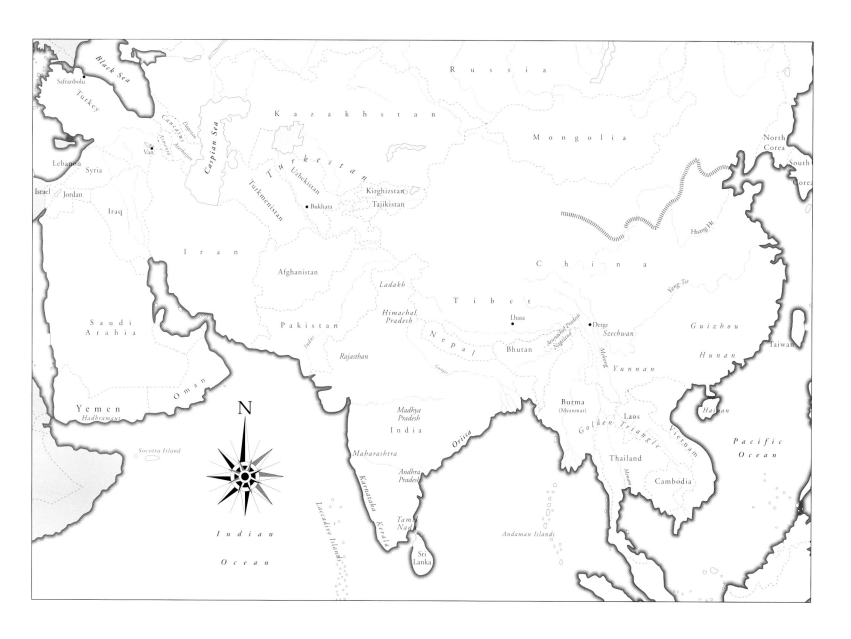

Black Sea

Safranbolu

Turkey

Caspian Sea

Caucasus

Dagestan

Azerbaijan

Armenia

Van

Lebanon

Syria

Israel

Jordan

Iraq

Iran

KAZAKHSTAN

RUSSIA

MONGOLIA

North
Corea

South
Corea

Turkestan

Turkmenistan

Uzbekistan

Bukhara

Kirghizstan

Tajikistan

Huang He

Afghanistan

CHINA

Ladakh

Tibet

Yang-Tse

Saudi
Arabia

Himachal
Pradesh

Lhasa

Derge

Szechwan

Guizhou

Pakistan

Nepal

Bhutan

Arunachal Pradesh

Nagaland

Hunan

Taiwan

Oman

Rajasthan

Indus

Ganges

Mekong

Yunnan

Yemen

Hadhramaut

Madhya
Pradesh

India

Burma
(Myanmar)

Golden Triangle

Laos

Vietnam

Hainan

Pacific
Ocean

N

Socotra Island

Maharashtra

Orissa

Thailand

Mekong

Indian

Andhra
Pradesh

Karnataka

Kerala

Tamil
Nadu

Andaman Islands

Cambodia

Laccadive Islands

Ocean

Sri
Lanka

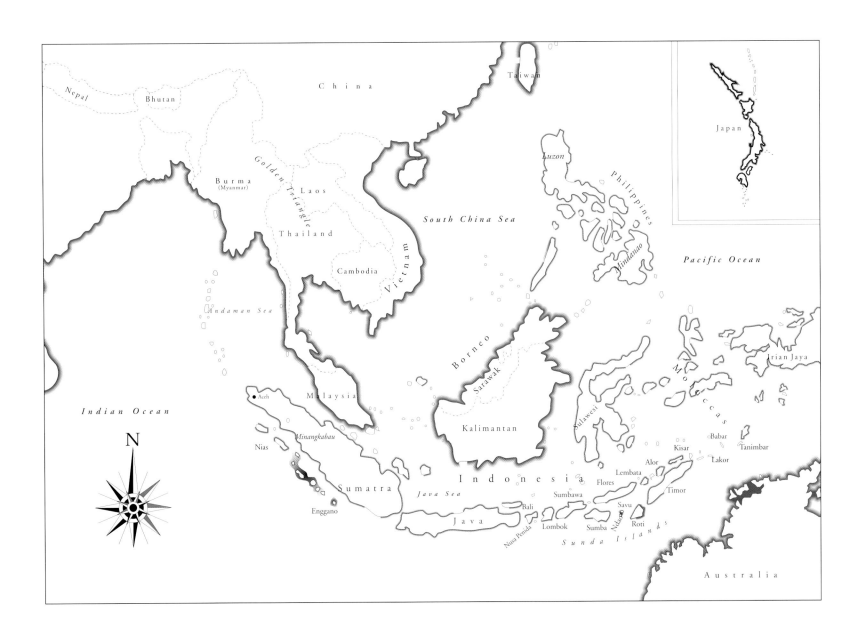

Nepal
Bhutan
China
Taiwan

Japan

Burma
(Myanmar)
Golden Triangle
Laos
Thailand
Cambodia
Vietnam
South China Sea
Luzon
Philippines
Mindanao
Pacific Ocean

Andaman Sea

Indian Ocean

Aceh
Malaysia
Borneo
Sarawak
Kalimantan
Sulawesi
Moluccas
Irian Jaya

N

Nias
Minangkabau

Sumatra
Java Sea
Indonesia
Babar
Kisar
Lakor
Tanimbar
Alor
Lembata
Flores
Timor

Enggano

Java
Bali
Sumbawa
Savu
Lombok
Sumba
Ndao
Roti
Nusa Penida
Sunda Islands

Australia

308

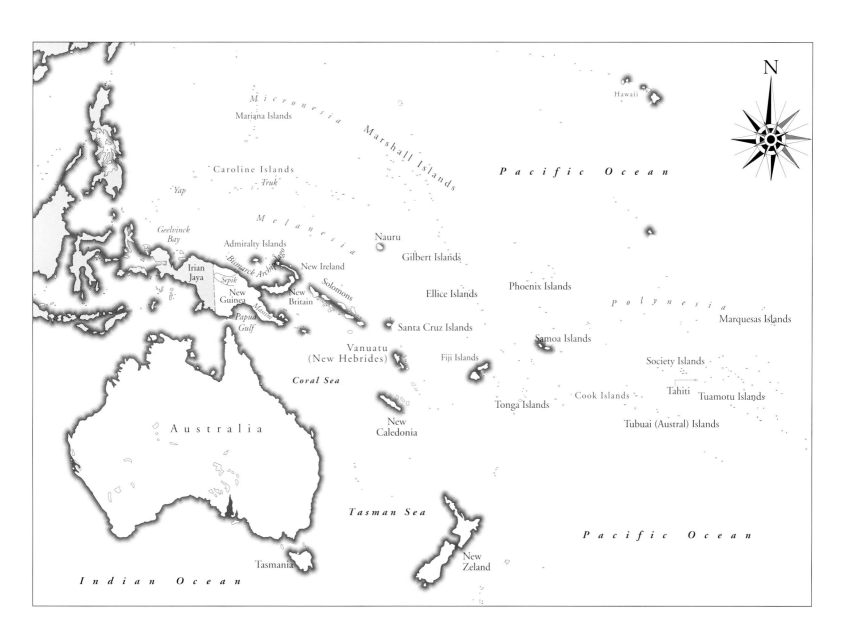

N

Micronesia

Mariana Islands

Marshall Islands

Caroline Islands

Truk

Yap

Pacific Ocean

Hawaii

Melanesia

Nauru

Geelvinck
Bay

Admiralty Islands

Bismarck Archipelago

New Ireland

Irian
Jaya

Sepik

Solomons

New Guinea

New
Britain

Massim

Papua
Gulf

Gilbert Islands

Ellice Islands

Phoenix Islands

Polynesia

Marquesas Islands

Santa Cruz Islands

Samoa Islands

Vanuatu
(New Hebrides)

Fiji Islands

Society Islands

Coral Sea

Tahiti

Tuamotu Islands

Cook Islands

Tonga Islands

Tubuai (Austral) Islands

New
Caledonia

Australia

Tasman Sea

Pacific Ocean

Tasmania

New
Zeland

Indian Ocean

309

Alaska

Great Lakes

United States

Arizona

New Mexico

Mexico

Guatemala

Caribbean Sea

Venezuela

Colombia

Guyana

Suriname

Fr. Guyana

Ecuador

Amazon River

Amazonia

Peru

Ucayali River

Xingu

Mato Grosso

Brazil

Bolivia

Pacific Ocean

Paraguay

Atlantic Ocean

Chile

Argentina

Uruguay

N

Glossary

Aluminium
A light, shiny, malleable metal which does not oxidize. Obtained in traditional societies by melting down imported domestic implements. Appreciated for its light weight.

Amulet
A piece of jewellery or object worn because it is believed to offer protection against evil, disease, etc. due to its shape, material or decoration.

Artefact
An object produced by human art or workmanship.

Betel
A mixture of tobacco, betel-nut, lime and spices rolled in the leaves of a climbing pepper and chewed as a stimulant. Called *paan* in India.

Brass
A yellow alloy based on copper and zinc.

Bronze
An alloy of copper and tin.

Chasing
A relief decoration on the surface of sheet or solid metal, which, unlike engraving, does not remove any material. The work is done with small chisels which are held at right angles to the metal and struck with a hammer. The cold metal is placed on a soft surface during chasing.

Chatelaine
A belt decoration on which jewels and small items are attached by a chain.

Copper
A ductile, malleable reddish brown metal easily attacked by acids. It can be worked with a hammer in its pure state or in an alloy.

Enamel
A vitreous material composed of a colourless, transparent crystalline base and colourants, usually metal oxides.

Enamelling
Application of opaque or translucent enamel on a gold, silver or copper base using specific procedures for each type of metal.

Fassi
A person living in Fez, one of Morocco's four imperial cities.

Filigree
Gold, silver or silver gilt wire used to make patterns. Used singly or in groups, they are twisted into patterns then welded to the metal base. When welded together they make openwork decorations. They can be enriched with granules or beads.

Forging
The shaping of red-hot metal. The object is forged by beating it with a hammer on an anvil.

Gilding
A thin layer of gold, especially gold leaf, laid on a metal base.

Glass beads
Beads or cabochons of coloured glass of various sizes, sometimes imitating precious stones.

Glass paste
A transparent glass powder to which coloured oxides are added to make a colourful, opaque glass paste.

Gold
A ductile, rustproof metal that withstands acid. It is used as gold leaf, drawn into wires or melted as granules. It can be chased, engraved, enamelled, nielloed and inlaid. It is highly malleable and is often used with other metals.

Granulation
Decorative technique using minute balls of metal, gold or silver. They are welded to a base of the same metal. Granulation is often used with filigree work.

Inro
A Japanese word for a small box containing seals, medicines or other small items, usually lacquered and decorated with various patterns.

Intan
An Indonesian word for a diamond.

Iron
A ductile but strong metal which is forged when hot and worked when cold. It corrodes in damp air, forming rust.

Lacquer
A reddish brown resin obtained from several eastern plants, for example the *Rhus vernicifera* tree. Commonly used in China and Myanmar.

Lion of Fo (also called Dog of Fo or Shih-Shih)
A mythical animal, like a lion, which is often placed outside temples in China.

Lost-wax casting
The molten metal takes the place of the wax model. As the model is destroyed during casting, each object is unique.

Netsuke
A Japanese word for a counterweight for items attached to a belt such as the inro or a tobacco pouch. Its decoration may be abstract, zoomorphic, anthropomorphic, etc.

Niello
Niello is a black substance made from an alloy of powdered copper, silver, lead and sulphur. The paste is pressed into fine grooves engraved in the metal base and then heated with a flux, so that it is fused into the grooves and gives strong colour contrasts. It is mainly used with gold and silver.

Obi
Japanese word for the sash tied at the back to secure a kimono.

Obidome
Japanese word for the ornament which slides along the *obijime* on two small hooks at the back. It takes many different forms.

Obijime
Japanese word for the woven silk ribbon which holds the obi in place.

Parka
Eskimo word for a waterproof hooded jacket. The Inuit (Eskimos) often make their parkas from sealskin or caribou skin.

Peplos
Greek word for a woman's woollen garment which is draped about the body and secured at the waist with a belt.

Sari
A Hindi word referring to a woman's garment worn in India; made up of a long piece of cloth with no seams or fastenings, it is draped around the body.

Setting
Assembling and securing stones or other materials in a metal base.

Silver
A metal found in mining deposits either as pure silver or mixed with other metals such as gold, copper, lead and zinc.

Silver gilt
Gilded silver.

Suasa
Indonesian word for an alloy of gold and copper.

Tapa
Polynesian word for a beaten bark cloth.

Toggle
English word for the equivalent of the japanese *netsuke*.

Wire
Metal wire is obtained by hammering or by drawing. The calibre of the cross-section varies. When twisted it can be used as a surface decoration.

Index

A

Abor 13
ACEH, kingdom of 109, 298, 299
Achuar 242
ADMIRALTY ISLANDS 300
AFGHANISTAN 291
AFRICA 7, 281
Ait Ouaouzguite 12
ALASKA 260, 302
ALOR 299
Amanab 300
AMAZON 242, 260
　　Achuar 242
AMAZON DELTA 260, 302
AMAZON FOREST 7
AMAZONIA 302, 303
AMERICA 260, 302
ANATOLIA 8
　　Central 8
ANDAMAN ISLANDS 7, 107, 293
　　Jarawa 7
　　Jawara 293
ANDHRA PRADESH 292
ANGKOR VAT 108
Apsara, sacred dancers 108
ARABIAN PENINSULA 106, 297
Arapesh 7, 242
ARIZONA 302
ARMENIA 106, 290
ARUNACHAL PRADESH 292
ASIA 8, 289
ATLANTIC OCEAN 12, 281
Aymara 302
AZERBAIJAN 106, 290, 291
　　Kabardinians 290
　　Tartars 290

B

Bagobo 109, 297
Bai 295
Baining 300
BALKANS 289
Bambuti Pygmies 286

Bamileke 284
Bamum 12
BANKS ISLANDS 243
Batak 109, 299
Baule 281
benyop 292
Berber 12, 281
Berbers 8
Besancenot, Jean 12
BHUTAN 293
BLACK SEA 106
BOHEMIA 293
BOLIVIA 302
　　Aymara 302
bolo 298
Bontoc 109, 297
Borana 285
BORNEO 7, 297
　　Dayak 7
　　Iban Dayak 109, 299
Botticelli, Sandro Filipepi
　　known as 242
　　Birth of Venus 242
BRAZIL 8, 260, 302, 303
　　Amazonia 302, 303
　　Kaiapo 8, 260, 261, 303
　　Mato Grosso 8, 303
　　Nambikwara 8
　　Panoan 302
　　Ucayali River 302
　　Xingu 303
BRITTANY 242, 293
Buddha 295
Bugis 299
BUKHARA 106, 290, 291
BURKINA FASO 8
　　Winié 8
Bushmen 14, 287
Bwaka 286
bwami, secret society 8, 13, 286

C

CAMBODIA 108
　　Angkor Vat 108

CAMEROON 8, 12, 282, 283, 284
　　Bamileke 284
　　Kapsiki 283
　　Kirdi 8, 12, 282, 283, 284
　　Mandara 12, 283
　　Matakam 283, 284
　　Tikar-Bamunka 283
CAROLINE ISLANDS 243, 300
　　Truk 300
　　Yap 300
CASPIAN SEA 106
CAUCASUS 8, 106, 290
CENTRAL AFRICA 12, 286
CENTRAL ASIA 106
Ch'ing, dynasty 294
CHAD 284
　　Mundang 284
Chang 293
CHILE 302
CHINA 14, 106, 108, 289, 294, 295, 296, 297, 299, 301
　　Bai 295
　　Ch'ing, dynasty 294
　　Dali 295
　　Han, dynasty 294
　　Miao 295
　　Szechwan 295
　　Warring States period 294
　　Yao 297
　　Yi 295
　　Yunnan 295
Chinese Taoist philosophy 294
concha 260, 302
CONGO, D.R. of 8, 13, 109, 281, 285, 286, 287
　　Bambuti Pygmies 286
　　Bwaka 286
　　Ituri 13, 286
　　Kuba 12, 286, 287
　　Lega 8, 13, 109, 286
　　Luba 285, 287
　　Lukuga 287
　　Luluwa 8, 13

Mangbetu 8, 12, 13, 285
Mbole 281, 285
Mongo 8, 13, 281
Wagenia 286
Courbet, Gustave 242
　　The Origin of the World 242
CROSS RIVER 282
Cuanhama 13, 287

D

DAGESTAN 106, 291
DALI 295
Dapper, Olfert 283
Dayak 7
de Bougainville, Louis-Antoine 242
　　Voyage autour du monde 242
DERGE 293
Dogon 12

E

EAST AFRICA 13
Ekonda 13
EQUATORIAL AFRICA 12
Eskimos 260
ESSAOUIRA 281
ETHIOPIA 284
　　Wollo 284
EUROPE 282, 284

F

Fassi 281
Fatima, the daughter of the Prophet 281
fekroun 281
FEZ 12, 281
FLORES 109
fon 12
futa 12, 281
FRANCE 294
FRENCH GUYANA 302
　　Wai Wai 302
Fulbe 12, 283

G

Gaddang 298
Gallong 13
galuchat 294
Gauguin, Paul 242
Gaulim 300
Gayo-Alas 298
Geelvinck Bay 242, 243, 301
Genghis Khan 106
Georgia 106
Georgians 290
Golden Triangle 297
Griaule, Marcel 7, 12

H

Hadhramaut 289
Han, dynasty 294
Héritier, Françoise 13
hezam 281
High Atlas 12
High Sepik 300
Himachal Pradesh 292
Himalayas 107
Himba 13, 287
Hindu 291, 299
holga 281
huaka 302
Huila 13

I

Iban Dayak 109, 299
Ifugao 109, 298
ijogolo 14, 288
Ilongot 297
India 8, 13, 14, 106, 107, 108,
   291, 292, 293, 297, 299,
   301
   Andaman Islands 7, 107,
      293
   Andhra Pradesh 292
   Arunachal Pradesh 292
   Chang 293
   Gallong 13
   Himachal Pradesh 292

Jawara 293
Karnataka 291
Kashmir 108
Kerala 291, 292
Khond 292
Konyak 293
Ladakh 108, 293
Madhya Pradesh 291
Maharashtra 291, 292
Naga 107, 293
Nagaland 293
Orissa 292
Sema 293
Tamil Nadu 292
Indian Ocean 7, 289, 293
Indonesia 108, 292, 298, 299,
   301
   Aceh, kingdom of 109, 298,
      299
   Alor 299
   Batak 109, 299
   Borneo 7, 297
   Dayak 7
   Flores 109
   Gayo-Alas 298
   Geelvinck Bay 301
   Irian Jaya 301
   Java 298, 299
   Kalimantan 109, 301
   Minangkabau 298
   Moluccas 109, 299
   Nias 109, 299
   Palembang 109
   Sulawesi 109, 297, 299
   Sumatra 109, 298, 299
   Sumba 109
   Toraja 109, 299
Indonesian Islands 299
inro 108, 296
intan 299
Inuit 302
Irian Jaya 301
Iroquois 260
isiphephethu 14

Ituri 286
Ivory Coast 281
   Baule 281
iyol 287

J

jambiya 106
Japan 7, 108, 294, 296
Jarawa 7
Java 298, 299
Jawara 293
jempang 299
Jivaro 260
jom 242

K

Kabardinians 290
Kaiapo 8, 260, 261, 303
Kalahari Desert 14
Kalimantan 109, 301
kama sutra 107
kanyamwa ke idul 286
kap kap 109
Kapsiki 283
Karnataka 291
Kashmir 108
Kenya 13, 284, 285
   Borana 285
   Masai 13, 285, 287
   Masai-Chamus 284
   Rendille 285
   Turkana 13
Kerala 291, 292
khan, nomadic chieftain 106,
   290
Khmer 108
Khond 292
Kirdi 8, 12, 282, 283, 284
Kirgiz 291
Klee, Paul 13
komia 12
Konyak 293
kraton 299
Kuba 12, 286, 287

Kuba, kingdom 8, 12
Kyrgyzstan 291

L

Lacan, Jacques 242
Ladakh 108, 293
Laos 108
Lega 8, 13, 109, 286
Lhasa 107
ligabi 14, 288
lipotho 14, 288
Luba 285, 287
Lukuga 287
Luluwa 8, 13
Luzon 109, 297, 298

M

Madhya Pradesh 291
Maharashtra 291, 292
Mahdia 281
Malakula 242
Malawi 287
   Yao 287
Malay Archipelago 108, 109,
   297, 299
Malay Peninsula 298
Malaysia 109, 292, 298, 299,
   301
   Iban Dayak 109, 299
   Sarawak 109, 299, 301
Malinowski, Bronislaw 242
Malo 242
Mandara mountains 12, 283
Manet, Édouard 242
   Olympia 242
Mangbetu 8, 13, 285
Mangbetu kingdom 12, 13
marfazah 289
Marquesas 242
Marrakech 12
Masai 13, 285, 287
Masai-Chamus 284
Masson, André 242
Matakam 283, 284

Mato Grosso 8, 303
Mbole 281, 285
Mbuti pygmies 13
Mead, Margaret 7, 242
Mediterranean Sea 12
Meknes 12
Melanesia 242, 243
    Banks Islands 243
    Malakula 242
    Malo 242
    New Guinea 7, 8, 242, 260, 300
    Solomon Islands 243, 300
Meru, sacred mountain 107, 108, 291
Meso-America 260
Miao 295
Minangkabau 298
Mindanao 109, 297
    Bagobo 109
Mogador (now called Essaouira) 281
Moluccas 109, 299
Mongo 8, 13, 281
Mongolia 108, 294, 295, 296
Mongolian culture 108
Moon ritual dance 260
moran 285
Morocco 12, 281
    Essaouira 281
    Fez 12, 281
    Marrakech 12
    Meknes 12
    Rabat 12
    Tafilalet 12
Mozambique 287
Mpande, Zulu king 14
mubangu 13
Mumuye 282
Mundang 284
Mundugumor 7
Muslim Fulbe 12, 283
Myanmar (formerly Burma) 108, 297

Padaung 297
Pyu period 297
Shan 108, 297

N
Naga 299
Naga 107, 293
Nagaland 293
Nambikwara 8
Namibia 13, 287
    Cuanhama 13, 287
    Himba 13, 287
    Huila 13
nassa 301
Navajo 260, 302
Ndebele 8, 14, 288
negbe 13, 285
netsuke 108, 295, 296
New Britain 300
New Guinea 7, 8, 242, 260, 300
New Ireland 109
New Mexico 302
Nguni 14
Nias 109, 299
Niger 283
    Peul 283
Nigeria 8, 282, 283, 284
    Cross River 282
    Kirdi 8
    Mumuye 282
    Vere 282, 283
Nogaians 290
North Africa 8, 12
North America 260
Northern India 291
Northern Irian Jaya 301
ntchak 286

O
obi 7, 296
obidome 296
obijime 296
Oceania 242, 300

omakipa 13, 287
Oman, Sultanate of 106, 289
Oppi Untracht 107
Orissa 292

P
Pacific Islands 300
Pacific Ocean 287
Padang 298
Padaung 297
Palembang 109
pandiëng 298
Panoan 302
Papua New Guinea 300
    Admiralty Islands 300
    Amanab 300
    Baining 300
    Gaulim 300
    High Sepik 300
    New Britain 300
Peul 283
Philippines 109, 297, 298
    Bagobo 109, 297
    Bontoc 109, 297
    Gaddang 298
    Ifugao 109, 298
    Ilongot 297
    Luzon 109, 297, 298
    Mindanao 109, 297
    Surigao 109
    T'Boli 297
Plains Indians 260, 302
Portuguese 298
Pumupud, goddess 298
Pygmies 13, 286, 293
Pyu period 297

Q
Queen Victoria 298

R
Rabat 12
Ramayana 107
Rendille 285

S
sabitan 297
Safranbolu 289
Samburu 13
Samoa 7
San 14, 287
sangilot 109
Sarawak 109, 299, 301
    Iban Dayak 109, 299
Second World War 287
Sema 293
Sfax 281
Shan 108, 297
Siddhartha Gautama 297
Socotra Island 289
Solomon Islands 243, 300
Sotho 287, 288
South Africa 8, 13, 14, 286, 287, 288
    Bushmen 287
    Ndebele 8, 14, 288
    San 287
    Sotho 287, 288
    Transvaal 288
    Xhosa 288
    Zulu 14, 287, 288
South America 260
South India 108, 291, 299, 301
Southeast Asia 8, 108, 242
South Seas 293
Spanish 302
Sri Lanka 292, 298, 299
stridhana 106, 291
suasa 298, 299
Sulawesi 109, 297, 299
Sumatra 109, 298, 299
    Aceh 109, 298, 299
    Batak 109, 299
    Minangkabau 298
    Padang 298
    Palembang 109
Sumba 109
Sun ritual dance 260

SURIGAO 109
SZECHWAN 295

T
TAFILALET 12
TAHITI 242
Tamerlane 290
TAMIL NADU 292
tanga 260, 302
tapa 300
Tartars 290
T'Boli 297
Tchambuli 7
tchapan 290
THAILAND 108, 297
    Yao 297
TIBET 107, 293, 294, 295
    Derge 293
    Lhasa 107
Tibetan culture 108
tikam 109
Tikar-Bamunka 283
Timurid, dynasty 291
TOGO 282
tolus ka towangan, protecting
    spirit 297
Toraja 109, 299
TRANSVAAL 288
    Ndebele 288
TROBRIAND 242
TRUK 300
TUNISIA 12, 281
    Mahdia 281
    Sfax 281
Turkana 13
TURKEY 106, 289, 290
    Safranbolu 289
    Van 290
TURKMENISTAN 106

U
UCAYALI RIVER 302
UNITED STATES 302
    Alaska 260, 302

Arizona 302
Navajo 206, 302
New Mexico 302
Plains Indians 302
West of the Great Lakes
    302
Zuni 302
upud 109, 298
urku 302
UZBEKISTAN 106, 290, 291
    Bukhara 290, 291
    Nogaians 290

V
VAN 290
VENICE 282, 299
Vere 282, 283
VIETNAM 108
von Plessen, baron Victor 7

W
Wagenia 286
Wai Wai 302
Warring States period 294
WEST AFRICA 12
WEST OF THE GREAT LAKES 302
Winié 8
WOLLO 284
woot 13

X
Xhosa 288
XINGU 303

Y
yang 294
Yao 287, 297
YAP 300
YEMEN 106, 289
    Hadhramaut 289
    Socotra Island 289
yet 286, 287
Yi 295
yin 294

yoni 107, 292
YUNNAN 295

Z
Zulu 14, 287, 288
Zuni 302

Bibliography

General Bibliography

Aethiopia, Peuples d'Éthiopie, Musée royal de l'Afrique centrale, Tervuren, 1996 (exhibition catalogue).

Bastin M.L., *Introduction aux Arts d'Afrique noire*, Arts d'Afrique Noire, Arnouville, 1984.

Bijoux ethniques, d'Afrique, d'Asie et des îles du Pacifique, Picquier, Paris, 2002.

Borel F., *The Splendor of Ethnic Jewelry. From the Colette and Jean-Pierre Ghysels Collection*, Harry N. Abrams, Inc., New York, 1994.

Ethnic Jewellery, ed. John Mack, Harry N. Ambrams Inc., New York, 1988 (also published by British Museum Press, London, 1994).

Geoffroy-Schneiter B., *Parures ethniques. Le culte de la beauté*, Assouline, Paris, 2001.

Hasson R., *Early and Later Islamic Jewelry*, L.A. Mayer Institute for Islamic Art, Jerusalem, 1987.

Héritier F., *Masculin/Féminin. La pensée de la différence*, Odile Jacob, Paris, 1996.

Malinowski, B., Sexuality and Repression in Savage Societies, Routledge and Kegan Paul, London, 1927 (reprint 1953).

Malinowski B., *Argonauts of the Western Pacific: An Account of Native Enterprise and Adventure in the Archipelagoes of Melanesian New Guinea,* E.P. Dutton & Co. Inc., New York, 1922; Waveland Press, Prospect Heights, Ill., reprint 1984.

Mead M., *Mœurs et sexualité en Océanie*, Coll. Terre humaine, Plon, Paris, reprint 1963. Eng. ed.: *Sex and temperament in Three Primitive Societies*, 1935; reprint the New American Library, New York, 1950.

Africa

Adamson J., *The Peoples of Kenya*, Collins & Harvill Press, London, 1967.

Au fil de la parole, Musée Dapper, Paris, 1995.

Benfoughal T., Bijoux et bijoutiers de l'Aurès, Algérie. Traditions & innovations, CNRS, Paris, 1997.

Besancenot J., *Costumes du Maroc, La Croisée des Chemins*, Édisud, Aix-en-Provence, reprint 2000.

Bijoux et parures d'Algérie, Somogy Éditions d'Art, Paris, 2003 (exhibition catalogue).

Coquet M., *Textiles africains*, Adam Biro, Paris, 1998.

Cornet J., *Art royal kuba*, Edizioni Sipiel, Milan, 1982.

Garrard T., *Gold of Africa: Jewellery and Ornaments from Ghana, Côte d'Ivoire, Mali and Senegal in the Collection of the Barbier-Mueller Museum*, Prestel, Munich and Musée Barbier-Mueller, Geneva, 1989.

Gebauer P., *Art of Cameroon*, The Portland Art Museum, Oregon and the Metropolitan Museum of Art, New York, 1979.

Ghysels, Eric, *La parure perlée chez les Ndebele*, degree dissertation, Université Libre de Bruxelles, 1986–87.

Ginzberg M., *Afrique. L'art des formes*, Skira/Seuil, Milan, 2000.

Grammet I., De Meersman M., *et al.*, *Splendeurs du Maroc*, Musée royal de l'Afrique centrale, Tervuren, 1998 (exhibition catalogue).

Griaule M., *Dieu d'eau. Entretiens avec Ogotemmêli*, Fayard, Paris, reprint 1966.

Kennedy C., *The Art and Material Culture of the Zulu-Speaking Peoples*, UCLA, Museum of Cultural History, 1978.

Mangbetu. *Art de cour africain de collections privées belges*, Kredietbank, Brussels, 1992 (exhibition catalogue).

Nooter Roberts M. and Roberts A.F.*, Memory. Luba Art and the Making of History*, Prestel, Munich and The Museum for African Art, New York, 1996.

Rabaté J. and M.-R., *Bijoux du Maroc. Du Haut-Atlas à la vallée du Draa*, Édisud/Le Fennec, Aix-en-Provence, 1996.

Rouach D., *Bijoux berbères au Maroc dans la tradition judéo-arabe*, ACR Édition, Paris, 1989.

Sugier Cl., *Bijoux tunisiens. Formes et symboles*, Cérès Productions, Tunis, 1977.

ubuntu. Arts et cultures d'Afrique du Sud, Éditions de la Réunion des musées nationaux, Paris, 2002 (exhibition catalogue).

Van der Stappen X., *Les Maasaï*, Renaissance du Livre, Tournai, 2002.

Asia

Bernard P. and Huteau M., *Yunnan-Guizhou. Couleurs tribales de Chine*, Anako Edition, Xonrupt-Longemer, 1989.

Boyer M., *Mongol Jewelry*, Thames and Hudson, London, 1995.

Casey Singer J., *Bijoux en or du Tibet et du Népal*, Olizane, Geneva, 1996.

Gabriel H., *Jewelry of Nepal*, Thames and Hudson, London 1999.

Heissig W. and Müller C.C., *Die Mongolen*, Pinguin Verlag, Innsbruck, Umschau-Verlag, Frankfurt.

Jacobs J., et al., *The Nagas. Hill People of North-East India: Society, Culture and the Colonial Encounter*, Thames and Hudson, London and New York, 1991

Lewis P. and E., *People of the Golden Triangle: Six Tribes in Thailand*, Thames and Hudson, London, 1984.

Morris M. Shelton P., *Oman Adorned. A Portrait of Silver*, Apex Publishing, Muscat and London, 1997.

Richter A., *The Jewelry of South-East Asia*, Thames and Hudson, London, 2000.

Rodgers S., *Power and Gold. Jewelry from Indonesia, Malaysia and the Philippines from the Collection of the Barbier-Müller Museum*, The Barbier-Müller Museum, Geneva, 1985, reprint: Prestel Publishing Ltd., London, 1988.

Ross H.C., *The Art of Bedouin Jewellery. A Saudi Arabian Profile*, Arabesque Commercial S.A., Fribourg, 1981.

Rossi G., *The Dong People of China. A Hidden Civilization*, Hagley & Hoyle Pte Ltd., Singapore, 1991.

Shizhao K., et al., *Clothings and Ornaments of China's Miao Peo-*

ple, The Cultural Palace of Nationalities, Beijing, 1985.

The Caucasian Peoples, Hessenhuis, Antwerp, 2001 (exhibition catalogue).

Untracht O., *Traditional Jewelry of India*, Thames and Hudson, London, 1997.

Oceania

La découverte de la Polynésie, Musée de l'Homme, Société des Amis du Musée de l'Homme, Paris, 1972 (exhibition catalogue).

La découverte du paradis. Océanie. Curieux navigateurs et savants, Musées du Nord-Pas-de-Calais, Somogy Éditions d'Art, Paris, 1997.

Le voyage de la Korrigane dans les mers du Sud, Musée de l'Homme, Hazan, Paris, 2001, (exhibition catalogue).

Meyer A.J.P., *Oceanic Art, Ozeanische Kunst, Art Océanien*, Könemann, Cologne, 1995.

Stöhr W., *Kunst und Kultur aus der Südsee, Sammlung Clausmeyer*, Rautenstrauch-Joest-Museum für Völkerkunde, Cologne, 1987.

Vanuatu, Océanie. Arts des îles de cendre et de corail, Réunion des Musées nationaux, Paris, 1996 (exhibition catalogue).

America

Dubin S., *North American Indian Jewelry and Adornment from Prehistory to the Present*, Harry N. Abrams Inc., New York, 1999.

Hartmann G., *Gold & Silber, Gold der Kuna, Panama, Silberschmuck der Mapuche, Chile*, Dietrich Reimer Verlag, Berlin, 1988.

Hurault J.M., *Indiens de Guyane, Wayana et Wayampi de la forêt*, Autrement, Paris, 2003.

The Ancient Americas Art from Sacred Landscapes, The Art Institute of Chicago, Prestel Verlag, Munich, 1992.

Verswijver G., *Kaiapo, Amazonie. Plumes et peintures corporelles*, Musée royal de l'Afrique centrale, Tervuren, 1992.

Viatte G., 'Les curiosités d'un collectionneur', in *Magazine Littéraire*, special issue no. 5; Lévi-Strauss, 'L'ethnologie ou la passion des autres', no. 5, 2003, pp. 43-5.